We Are the Bride
SERIES

ORGANIC CHRISTIANITY: BACK TO THE GARDEN

#2 in WATB Series

TreeHouse
Publishers

Author
Dr. June Dawn Knight

This book is the twin book to
Clarion Call to UNITY in the Bride of Christ.
According to prophecy, these books are meant to be together.

Copyright © 2016 Dr. June Dawn Knight

All rights reserved.

TreeHouse Publishers
ISBN-13: 978-0692653791
ISBN-10: 0692653791

DEDICATION

This book is dedicated to the Bride of Christ as Book #2 in the We are the Bride Series. This is a Twin Book to *Clarion Call to Unity in the Bride of Christ*. The Lord gave me a dream and said these books are twins and are meant to be together. February 2016.

This book is dedicated to the Holy Spirit who is my best friend! He is my revelator, teacher, comforter, correctional officer, etc. He is my guide on Earth and helped me to write this book. Without Him downloading all the revelations into my spirit, I would not have been able to impart it to the Bride. I am forever grateful for the relationship I have with my Creator!

I also dedicate this book to the wonderful church members of World Outreach Revival Center in Picayune, Mississippi. The whole town has just been wonderful and very welcoming. Thank you Pastor David Meeks for opening up your church to me and your members taking care of me while I birth these books into the world. Without your love and support, I could not have completed this assignment with the peace and grace I experienced. Thank you all.

Thank you to Ruth Powers for editing this book & housing!
Thank you to Jessica McKay for paying for the cover!
Thank you to Angelia Marable for your donations to help with books!
Thank you to Kreation Kings, LLC. for the cover!
Thank you to Bob & Joyce Guidry for the Little Cabin on the Hill!
Thank you to Sharon Joylea Davis for being my intercessor!

Additional Insight Included in this Book:

Apostle Pat Ehmann - Spiritual Mother – Hattiesburg, MS

Dr. Deven Cavalier - Watson, LA

Dr. Dianna Senkyrik –Spiritual Mother - Bay City, TX

Intercessor – Joyce Guidry - Spiritual Mother – Necaise, MS

Pastor Carolyn Sissom - Katy, TX

Pastor Mark Gambino – Picayune, MS

Pastor Marvin Adkins - Spiritual Father – Picayune, MS

Pastor Paul Taylor - Blythewood, SC

Prophetic Revivalist – Ron Teal – Spiritual Father – Hartselle, AL

Revivalist Timothy Lovett – Winfield, AL

Son Andrew Knight – Lancaster, OH

Son Brock Knight – Prattville, AL

Reviews:

After reading *Organic Christianity*, it shows the contrast of the original pure state of those in fellowship with God to those who are now confessing they know Him. There is too much fluff and stuff that has been intermingled with the pureness of worship and fellowship.

There is a great divide of the haves and have-nots. God is calling for unity so that we can realize that we've been called together as one body to supply the needs of the entire body.

Dr. June Knight goes deep into the core of the dysfunction of the church and plainly identifies the remedy for her ills.

I pray that it will touch many lives and challenge every reader to examine their lives and get back to an organic lifestyle of righteousness and heed the *Clarion Call for UNITY*. God bless you.

Pastor Angela Walker
Ministry of the True and Living God
La Vergne, Tennessee

This is truly direct from the mind of God and is a powerful weapon in the hands of the saints. Power eye-opening and life giving for your next level.

Bishop Witness Mswazi Dlamini
Healing Word Tabernacles International
Johannesburg South Africa

Do nothing from selfishness or empty conceit, but with humility of mind regard one another as more important than yourselves; do not merely look out for your own personal interests, but also for the interests of others.

Tree of Knowledge of Good & Evil

Please notice all the different forms of "Me" and "Self" in the Tree.

Table of Contents

INTRODUCTION 1

1 7

GOD'S PLAN FOR HUMANITY 7

A Quest for Relationship 7

Book of Remembrance and Destiny 14

God Loves Books! 14

Back to Our Book of Destiny and Remembrance 15

My Discovery of My Destiny & This Book 17

Angels on Assignment and the Books of Destiny 20

2 23

CREATION OF THE GARDEN 23

His Beautiful Creation 23

3 35

THE ULTIMATE GARDENER 35

The Creator as Ultimate Gardener 35

Leaves Blowing Away From Your Tree 38

Gardener Knows What He Is Doing 38

His Trees Have a Will and Choice in the Garden 41

4 43

GOD & RELATIONSHIP TO MAN 43

The Relationship Begins 43

God Became Daddy God & Protector 44

TREES & MAN TO GOD 46

God to the Trees & Humanity 49

God Speaks Through Dreams & Visions 54

5 57

THE TREE OF KNOWLEDGE 57

What Is This Tree? 57

Is This Tree Still Here? 58

How Do We Eat From This Tree Today? 59

Will This Tree Affect My Roots? 60

The Tree of Knowledge of Good and Evil Today 63

Too Much Knowledge Can Be Dangerous 65

6 67

TREE OF LIFE & LEAVES OF HEALING 67

Tree of Life 67

Leaves for Healing of the Nations 70

7 79

HUMANS ARE TREES? 79

How are we a Tree?.. 79

Salvation – A Supernatural Experience 81

Interesting Facts about Humans Compared to Trees:.................. 84

Our Trees Are Unique 87

A Hollow Tree/Evil Tree 88

Am I a Good or Bad Tree? 89

Two Trees Standing Before the Throne on Judgment Day 89

How Do You Take Care of Your Tree? 91

Dream About Sin in a Tree 92

We Are All Mighty Oaks.. 96

How Tree Comes to LIFE and.. 96

Connect to the Rivers of Living Water............................. 96

Dream - Finish the Race 97

Dream about Tree of Life.. 98

8 101

TYPES OF SEEDS IN THE GARDEN.................................. 101

You are the Conduit 101

Faith Seed 104

Financial Seeds.. 105

Family Trees and Seeds.. 107

Spiritual Seeds... 109

How Trees Release and Receive Seeds 110

9 119

GUARD THE GATES TO THE GARDEN 119

Sexual Gate 120

The Mouth Gate... 123

The Ear Gate.. 126

The Eye Gate.. 128

The Hand Gate 129

Heart Gate 130

Forgiveness of the Heart... 132

The Enemy; The Fox... 134

10 137

JESUS & THE GARDEN 137

Israel was God's Bride 138

The Church is Jesus' Bride 141

The Price of Jesus – The Betrothal 142

Dream About God Turning His Back on Jesus at Cross 145

Symbolism of Jesus Buried in Garden......................... 147

Jesus as Sacrifice for Us... 148

THE PRICE OF MAN – THE ACCEPTANCE......................... 149

Revelation about Time.. 150

11...155

THE HIDDEN GARDEN OF PRAYER & INTERCESSION 155

Our Secret Weapon 155

The Weapon of the Garden...157

Communication with our Creator......................................161

Eyes of God Stopped to Watch Me.....................................162

Praying in the Spirit Through Tongues 164

Worship as Intercession 167

Jesus in Intercession..168

Forgiveness in the Garden...172

Birthing in the Spirit 173

Birthing in We are the Bride Ministries 173

Birthing in the Garden Books...174

12 177

AN APPEAL TO HEAVEN 177

Revival in Your Tree...178

Strengthening Our Roots for Revival.................................180

REPENTANCE – Examine our Trees God! 183

Look at these pretty trees...184

13 193

ORGANIC CHRISTIANITY_BACK TO THE GARDEN 193

Trees That Have Been in the Storms – The Beaten Trees......... 194

14 199

DR. JUNE DAWN KNIGHT'S TREE 199

My LIFE as of 02/15/16 199

Dream of My Translucent Butterfly.......................... 208

15 209

PRAYER TO FIND THE GARDEN 209

WORKS CITED.. 211

ABOUT THE AUTHOR 215

INTRODUCTION

This book is a twin book with *Clarion Call to UNITY in the Bride of Christ.* They are meant to be together according to a dream the Lord gave me on February 2, 2016. He told me in the dream that they are twins. These books are "Book Ends." One represents the beginning, and the other represents the end. This book represents the beginning of time and our role back in the garden. The other book represents the end of time and is a prophetic book about days to come.

The *Clarion Call to UNITY* reveals the garden relationship we must have with God to endure the trials that are ahead. It examines the current-day church system and reveals to the Bride how we can have UNITY despite our differences. It talks about the Tree of Life and Jesus being the root of that tree. We are going to choose the right tree in the end and redeem mankind to God. We will be the generation that does not choose to satisfy SELF like Eve did. Thus, it may cost us our lives. However, by our choosing the Tree of Life in the end instead of accepting Satan's fruit in the end, we will have eternal life.

Organic Christianity: Back to the Garden reflects the need to go back to the garden and our roots to build a relationship with God that He has intended for us since the beginning of time. It's dropping all processed traditions, doctrines, beliefs, trainings, expectations, and culture. It's going back to our Creator and opening our hands wide and proclaiming, "Reveal yourself to me God! Show me your destiny for me and teach me how to please you with my life. Heal my roots, and make me whole again in your eyes." We are being transparent before God and allowing Him to examine our roots and do some housecleaning so that we can be used by Him. It's purity before a Holy God!

It's going from processed and tainted to the original intent of holiness and purity.

It's time for the Bride to clean her lamps for her soon-coming King! I pray this book encourages you to press forward knowing that YOU are His Bride.

As I minister in various prisons, I realize one of the greatest attacks of Satan upon the Church today is in our identity. Satan tries to convince the Church that its members do not have self-worth and attempts to distract them from their destiny and calling. If the Church does not have the revelation that they are the Bride of Christ with all rights to the inheritance that God has provided for them, they will not achieve the destiny that God designed for them before time began.

Over 51% of the prisoners in the United States are incarcerated due to drugs. Less than one percent is due to murder. The rest are due to identity crisis sins such as robbery, etc. These statistics are from prison training I've had in various prisons. I'm sure it's as shocking to you as it was for me.

I pray this book will open your eyes to God's true calling and purpose for your LIFE.

God specifically designed each human for a reason. The reason is to give humans a choice as to whether or not he will serve God. If a person CHOOSES to allow God to finish his LIFE destiny book, they will reveal another aspect of who God is to humanity.

We are all here to provide a revelation of who God is. One human may reveal how great His mercies are for mankind. Another may reveal how He is a healing God.

Another person may reveal how, if humanity trusts God, He will be the true husband and provider, etc. Each human has a divine reason for being on Earth.

2

When a person makes the choice to surrender his life to his Creator, we will then know that God can take anyone's nothingness and make it into something.

We are on Earth in God's Great Garden. This book delves into the Garden and how He created this beautiful place for us to respect and enjoy.

Like a tree in God's Great Garden, we are commanded to bear good fruit. If a tree bears good fruit, it is alive and well-nourished on the inside. If a tree does not bear fruit, it is withered and dry on the inside. We want to bear much fruit for the Kingdom of God.

This book also explores the various ways we taint our trees. It provides insight into the enemy's tactics to tempt you to receive of the fruit from the Tree of Knowledge of Good and Evil. It also brings revelation to the Tree of Life as our life-source today.

I pray that after reading this book, you will wake up every morning and recognize the birds, the beautiful trees, and the beautiful sky that God provides for you every day. He wants you to enjoy the garden that He has created for humanity.

Organic Christianity examines the heart of Christianity and declares that we are still in that garden as the True Bride. We must know our position in God and who and what we are in Christ, and He in us, so we can be confident no matter what the enemy may throw at us. We are a victorious Bride!

We are either going to burn on fire for God on Earth allowing our tree to bear all the fresh fruit for God that we can, or we will stand before God on judgment day and hear Him will say, "I gave your tree one chance on Earth to bear much fruit, and you did not even enjoy my garden.

"You did not enjoy the birds of the air and the beautiful trees I gave you, nor the landscape, the sky, and the time I gave you as a gift.

"You took your tree and became selfish and wanted to do with your tree what you wanted to do. I have no choice but to cast your tree into the fire. You were of no use to me on Earth."

> *Matthew 3:10 - The ax is already at the root of the trees and every tree that does not produce good fruit will be cut down and thrown into the fire.*

If you allow God to judge you on Earth, to keep your roots clean, and to receive His living water flowing through them, you will bear much godly fruit here on Earth. Thus, when you stand before the throne of God, God will look at your tree and say, "You did well in my garden! Now, go and enjoy eternity."

Life here on Earth is very short, so I pray that you will allow God to prune your tree, clean your roots, and purge your tree so that you can bear much good fruit for him on Earth. God bless you as you read this book.

Included is an excerpt from my autobiography. It's an extension, or continuation, of my first book: *Testimony of a Broken Bride, Jesus is the True Husband.* I share from my heart the struggles I've had in surrendering to God's perfect will for my life. God can take your negative and turn it into a positive!

1

GOD'S PLAN FOR HUMANITY

Have you ever wondered why we exist? Have you wondered why God takes us through tests and trials? Have you wondered how humanity began and the purpose of our existence on Earth? As we grow older, we see people come and go. We see lives tragically taken at young ages and others who live to be 110 years old, etc. Some lives seem to be fulfilled and rich in family and love, while others seem to be cold and indifferent. Why is that? Why does each of us experience God on different levels? It is because we each have a destiny that He wrote before time began. We are all unique in His eyes.

Before time began, a battle raged between the angels and God because of a chief archangel named Lucifer. Imagine how it hurt God when Lucifer, his chief angel and worship leader, turned his back on Him and turned 1/3 of the angels against Him. Why did Lucifer turn his back on God? The answer is pride. He thought he was better than God, and God had no choice but to throw him out of his presence because He cannot be around sin. Lucifer made a choice to reject God through his pride and ended up tainting God's angels. In order to prevent this from happening again, God created mankind.

A Quest for Relationship

God created the Earth after Lucifer's fall from Heaven. He created the Earth, the garden, and mankind for a reason.

One very important point we must all remember is that Lucifer (referred to as Satan) is not equal to God. (Prophetic Revivalist Ron Teal, January 2016, at the Hub Gathering in Hattiesburg, Mississippi) Lucifer is a fallen angel and always will be.

The battle that has been raging to this day is because Lucifer is still trying to turn people against God. How does he tempt humanity? His main weapon is pride. Think of how he did with Adam and Eve.

He tempted them with pride by explaining how they will have all-knowing power by eating of this tree. This is pride. God is triumphant and wins in the end!

By the time God created the Earth, His heart was to create people to have a relationship with Him, people who would choose Him over pride. It's almost like we are on Earth for a testing period to see how we choose to live which will determine our eternity. In this time period, we will be tested and tried to ensure that we have clean hearts to be in His Kingdom.

This is to prevent another disaster such as His experience with Lucifer. Did you know that Satan will be loosed one more time after the Millennium to tempt one more time?

It's almost like He began the stage for testing mankind. What do you do when you test something? You take your hypothesis and create an environment to test your theory. Then, He sits back and watches creation to see what we will choose and how we will do it. This is why He loves to discuss His actions with us. Before God judges the Earth, He reveals to His prophets. Look at this:

> *Amos 3:7 - Surely the Lord God will do nothing,*
> *but he revealeth his secret unto his servants the*
> *prophets.*

8

He informs His prophets so that they can reason together with Him and to warn mankind. He wants them to repent and plead with Him for mercy. Many times throughout history, God has changed His mind about pending actions due to the intercession of His people. It's all mercy by God to reveal His plans. If the people do not repent, He follows through. I'll give you a couple of examples:

Abraham talked to God about His impending destruction of Sodom and Gomorrah. God informed Abraham that He was destroying this city due to its sin. Abraham pleaded with God and shifted God's plan:

> *Genesis 18:16-33*
>
> *16 And the men rose up from thence, and looked toward Sodom: and Abraham went with them to bring them on the way.*
>
> *17 And the Lord said, Shall I hide from Abraham that thing which I do;*
>
> *18 Seeing that Abraham shall surely become a great and mighty nation, and all the nations of the earth shall be blessed in him?*
>
> *19 For I know him, that he will command his children and his household after him, and they shall keep the way of the Lord, to do justice and judgment; that the Lord may bring upon Abraham that which he hath spoken of him.*
>
> *20 And the Lord said, Because the cry of Sodom and Gomorrah is great, and because their sin is very grievous;*

21 I will go down now, and see whether they have done altogether according to the cry of it, which is come unto me; and if not, I will know.

22 And the men turned their faces from thence, and went toward Sodom: but Abraham stood yet before the Lord.

23 And Abraham drew near, and said, Wilt thou also destroy the righteous with the wicked?

24 Peradventure there be fifty righteous within the city: wilt thou also destroy and not spare the place for the fifty righteous that are therein?

25 That be far from thee to do after this manner, to slay the righteous with the wicked: and that the righteous should be as the wicked, that be far from thee: Shall not the Judge of all the earth do right?

26 And the Lord said, If I find in Sodom fifty righteous within the city, then I will spare all the place for their sakes.

27 And Abraham answered and said, Behold now, I have taken upon me to speak unto the Lord, which am but dust and ashes:

28 Peradventure there shall lack five of the fifty righteous: wilt thou destroy all the city for lack of five? And he said, If I find there forty and five, I will not destroy it.

29 And he spake unto him yet again, and said, Peradventure there shall be forty found there. And he said, I will not do it for forty's sake.

30 And he said unto him, Oh let not the Lord be angry, and I will speak: Peradventure there shall thirty be found there. And he said, I will not do it, if I find thirty there.

31 And he said, Behold now, I have taken upon me to speak unto the Lord: Peradventure there shall be twenty found there. And he said, I will not destroy it for twenty's sake.

32 And he said, Oh let not the Lord be angry, and I will speak yet but this once: Peradventure ten shall be found there. And he said, I will not destroy it for ten's sake.

33 And the Lord went his way, as soon as he had left communing with Abraham: and Abraham returned unto his place.

Abraham changed God's mind about Sodom. God ended up destroying the city, but He looked for the ten righteous and found only Lot & his family. He actually considered what Abraham said.

He doesn't have to because He is God. He can do what He wants.

Another example is Jonah. Jonah was told by God that He was destroying Nineveh. Jonah told Nineveh they're about to be destroyed in three days, and the city repented from the top down. The government proclaimed a fast and required that everyone participate.

After much crying and repenting, God changed His mind, which made Jonah angry.

Jonah 3:1-10

1 And the word of the Lord came unto Jonah the second time, saying,

2 Arise, go unto Nineveh, that great city, and preach unto it the preaching that I bid thee

3 So Jonah arose, and went unto Nineveh, according to the word of the Lord. Now Nineveh was an exceeding great city of three days' journey.

4 And Jonah began to enter into the city a day's journey, and he cried, and said, Yet forty days, and Nineveh shall be overthrown.

5 So the people of Nineveh believed God, and proclaimed a fast, and put on sackcloth, from the greatest of them even to the least of them.

6 For word came unto the king of Nineveh, and he arose from his throne, and he laid his robe from him, and covered him with sackcloth, and sat in ashes.

7 And he caused it to be proclaimed and published through Nineveh by the decree of the king and his nobles, saying, Let neither man nor beast, herd nor flock, taste any thing: let them not feed, nor drink water:

8 But let man and beast be covered with sackcloth, and cry mightily unto God: yea, let them turn every one from his evil way, and from the violence that is in their hands.

9 Who can tell if God will turn and repent, and turn away from his fierce anger, that we perish not?

10 And God saw their works, that they turned from their evil way; and God repented of the evil, that he had said that he would do unto them; and he did it not.

Following this forgiveness of Nineveh by God, Jonah became angry, and God threw him into the belly of a whale, etc. You probably know the rest of the story. However, the main point is that God relented and did not punish Nineveh, and it was based upon their repentance and heart. I will investigate God's relationship to man in another chapter.

Test of a Prophet
By: Ronald L. Dart
Why Should God Tell Us the Future?

Why on earth, after all, should God tell us anything about the future?

The only reason I can think of is, that He expects us to do something with the information, like repent, turn your life around, and straighten out your life and fly right. (Dart, 2011)

God help us to have prophets today to speak the truth to us and not tickle our ears! If we do not speak truth to the Bride, we do not truly love them. Love will tell the truth, even if it hurts.

13

Book of Remembrance and Destiny

God created EACH PERSON before time began. The Trinity wrote our destiny books.

> *Malachi 3:16 – Then they that feared the LORD spake often one to another: and the LORD hearkened, and heard it, and a book of remembrance was written before him for them that feared the LORD, and that thought upon his name.*
>
> *Exodus 32:32 Yet now, if thou wilt forgive their sin--; and if not, blot me, I pray thee, out of thy book which thou hast written.*
>
> *Psalm 56:8 Thou tellest my wanderings: put thou my tears into thy bottle: are they not in thy book?*
>
> *Psalm 69:28 - Let them be blotted out of the book of the living, and not be written with the righteous.*
>
> *Daniel 7:10 - A fiery stream issued and came forth from before him: thousand thousands ministered unto him, and ten thousand times ten thousand stood before him: the judgment was set, and the books were opened.*

God Loves Books!

Before I go any further, please let me point out that God loves books. There are many different types of books in Heaven. Everything we do and say is recorded in books. It's almost like we are participating in a virtual reality movie, and Heaven and Hell are watching the outcome.

Heaven is recording our actions in books so that we can be rewarded later. Hell is watching our actions, and if we provide an open door to sin, they will run through that door to destroy our destiny. Satan is a policeman. He is waiting for us to entertain thoughts and let that seed grow into sin.

They are also recording our words, and we will answer to God for how we used our tongues, which have much more power than we can imagine. We are created in God's image, and He created the whole Earth with His mouth. So, we are judged by how we used this power. The Bible says that the mouth speaks death and life, curses and blessings.

In addition to the recorded books, we have books written like the Lamb's Book of Life which records the names of the chosen ones. This book contains only the names of God's people, and only the Lamb, which was slain from the foundation of the Earth, is worthy to open that book. How holy is that? How awesome is that? Only our husband has the rights to open that book to present to His father!

Back to Our Book of Destiny and Remembrance

God has a book written about our time on Earth. God, the Trinity, wrote a story about each human to bring a revelation to mankind about the wonders of God. Each person is to reveal something different or another aspect of who God is.

The book content depends on the human's choices. If the human will die to his will once he gets saved and realize his identity in Christ, he will choose to give God the pen to his story and allow Him to finish that book the way He meant it to be.

God will then take over that book and reshape that story to create the most amazing, wonderful book to blow the human's mind, and the minds of those around him.

This book requires great patience, trust, obedience, relationship, love, continual dying of themselves, and time. We walk in obedience on a daily basis of faith. We walk one day at a time, trusting that God holds our tomorrow.

The choice remains. Will the human allow God to take the pen to their destiny and finish their earthly stories, or will he be selfish and keep the pen because he doesn't want to obey God and pay the price that He requires to continue the chapters?

Did you know that if you do not obey God at one chapter, you are literally stuck there and cannot continue to further chapters?

You will continue around that mountain over and over again until you learn your lesson or surrender that part of yourself to God. God is jealous over you and requires all of you. He will not quit either until you release that, or you just die in that state and staleness.

So many Christians die like this. They refuse to obey God on a certain thing, and they will never know what is on the other side of that thing until they obey.

Thus, most of them will probably die not knowing. They couldn't wait, got impatient, or just gave up within their spirits. The Bible says hope deferred makes the heart sick. We must keep our hope and encouragement in God.

Also, some ministers will be instructed by God to give up their ministries, to do this or do that, but they will not want to leave their comfortable ministries, face the consequences, or whatever it is that God is asking them to deny. They do not want to pay the price that God requires. They will continue doing other things to impress society, thinking they are really doing something.

However, doing all that good and disobeying God is not worth the labor or time. It's fruitless and worthless in God's eyes when it comes to your obedience.

Yes, God may use it because He always situations and people even when they don't have the right motives because He loves mankind. He will not honor your heart unless what was done was done with a right heart and in obedience. Obedience is always better than sacrifice!

All of we ministers know about the big name ministers who were caught in the sex scandals in the 80s. It damaged the church a lot at that time. Well, did you know that God gave some of them at least three opportunities to repent and turn from that sin before it was exposed?

God had mercy on them enough to warn them. He's not going to embarrass His Bride if they will stay humble and repent when confronted with sin (like David, etc.). He will provide grace for change. However, if we are prideful and resist God's requests, we will pay the consequences.

My Discovery of My Destiny & This Book

I'm writing all of this based upon my experience with God and obeying Him. I can tell you that when you do not obey Him, you will go through continual trouble and trials until you surrender.

In my case, after my first marriage ended, God insisted that He have me all to Himself because He was jealous over me. I said no because I didn't want to pay that price He required. I hesitated at the thought of celibacy and not having a husband. I was determined to keep the pen to my life. I didn't want to give Him that much control over me. Because of that decision, I married five more times and made a fool out of myself in my disobedience. He drove me to the ground to get me to surrender.

I went to the bottom before I could look up and say, "OK God, you can take the pen back, and I repent."

Even then, I became angry about how long God was taking to help me in a problem, and I took that pen back and started writing my chapters my way. I couldn't stand the suffering and watching my family suffer so I rescued us.

Seven years later when He backed me against a wall again, I again surrendered that pen. This time, He's deliberately kept that pen a long way from my reach and prevented me from even the temptation to grab it back. He also let me know that if I grabbed that pen and took control again, He would end the story.

So, now I know, it's ALL Him or nothing. Yes, He takes our stories serious. He is jealous over us!

Now that I see what He's doing with the pen to my life, I feel so goofy to even think about trying to make my destiny better than His! What? He's allowing me to marry again in the future. This time, **it** will be to the love of my life and in the right way?

What? He's going to restore my life to 1,000 times better than I could have ever dreamed? What? He's giving me a radio and television station in the future? He's giving me the media mountain? What? All I wanted for my life was a little home, a family, etc. His plan for me was so much better than I could have ever imagined.

When I was in one of those backslidden states, I was at a revival when an evangelist prayed for me. I went flying back and was laid out on the floor. (Most call it being slain in the spirit.)

While on the floor I went into an open vision:

I was standing before the throne of God. I saw my life flash before my eyes. However, it was not what I expected in that it was not a replay of my good and bad deeds.

18

It flashed up people before my eyes that had died and were affected by my life because I was not right with God.

The Lord said, "These are all the souls that went to Hell because of your decision to not follow my plan for your life."

I was rolling on the floor wanting to pull my hair out at the horror of what I had done and all those people who were affected by my decision to be selfish with my life! This one girl's face flashed before my eyes, and her memory came to my mind. She was a girl in our neighborhood whom my mother and I took to church.

Now, being that my mother and I were delivered from smoking, we urged her all the time to quit smoking. We didn't realize we were pressuring her. We often said things like, "You really need to quit smoking so that you can be all God wants you to be. You need to be victorious by quitting smoking." She replied, "I already gave up prostitution, drinking, and drugs. I am not ready to give these up." So, she eventually quit church. She only lasted about a month after that and died of a drug overdose. When we went to her funeral, it was so ice-cold that you just knew she went to Hell. You could feel the evil in the room. As I'm remembering this girl, I'm crying so hard asking God to forgive me.

I couldn't help but lay there and cry. I wept so hard before the Lord when I realized how my selfishness affected other souls.

Most of the people I saw in the vision I didn't even know! They were people I had never met because I was on the wrong course.

I encourage you to allow the Holy Spirit to search your heart today to see if there are areas of disobedience in your life and allow you to make things right with Him. He is real, and He wants to have a relationship with you.

Ask Him to reveal your heart to you and to help you repent and get on the right path.

It is only when we surrender our will to His that He can take our books and put us on the right path.

Allow Him to finish your book that He wrote before time began.

Angels on Assignment and the Books of Destiny

Charles and Frances Hunter wrote a book about Roland Buck's experience in Heaven with angels. They write about when he went to the throne room, and God showed him all the books of destiny. This is from that book:

In answer to my question, God let me see the vastness of his heavenly archives! My head swam! There was no way my finite mind could understand how God could keep track of these files.

There must be billions of them! He said, "Since you are overwhelmed by this, and it staggers you, let me pull out one that you can relate to." And he immediately pulled out mine! He would not let me see the contents of it, but mentioned a few of the future items listed which I could use as confirmation of this visit.

Then he did another very surprising thing! He wrote down 120 events which he said would happen in my life in the future.

It wasn't like you and I write; the information just suddenly appeared!

I did not even need to read it, but right now, I can tell you EVERYTHING that was on that paper, because it was instantly impressed on my mind like a printing press prints on paper. The press doesn't have to read what is imprinted. It's there!

In the same way, every single notation was burned into my mind, and it's still there!

Even though I had this knowledge, God also let me know that he did not want me to reveal any of these things until such times as he would release me to share them.

He said, "Let me show you someone else's record that you will easily understand."

He pulled out the file on Cyrus and reminded me of the last verse of Isaiah 44, and the first five verses of 45 where he said, "When I say of Cyrus, 'He is my shepherd,' he will certainly do as I say; and Jerusalem will be rebuilt and the Temple restored, for I have spoken it. "This is Jehovah's message to Cyrus, God's anointed, whom he has chosen to conquer many lands. God shall empower his right hand and he shall crush the strength of mighty kings. God shall open the gates of Babylon to him; the gates shall not be shut against him anymore. I will go before you, Cyrus, and level the mountains and smash down the city gates of brass and iron bars.

And I will give you treasures hidden in the darkness, secret riches; and you will know that I am doing this - I, the Lord, the God of Israel, the one who calls you by your name. "And why have I named you for this work? For the sake of Jacob, my servant - Israel, my chosen. I called you by name when you didn't know me" (TLB). God looked far into the future and saw exactly what was going to happen.

He allowed me to see the record books, and also his blueprints for many lives. One book was that of the apostle Paul. It revealed that he would be used to bring the Gospel to kings, rulers, and men of authority. For this reason,

21

God gave him a bigger brain capacity than normal, and because he was more brilliant, he caused him to study under the greatest teachers of his day, finally being tutored by Gamaliel, the most outstanding teacher of that time.

God had chosen Paul to write the Scripture, the Epistles, His plan for the church and His body, so he prepared him for this task. *(Hunter, 2002)*

Isn't that amazing how each human had his own book written, and it is documented? What does your book say?

2

CREATION OF THE GARDEN

His Beautiful Creation

When God created the Earth, it is very interesting how He did it. It was void and dark until He spoke things into existence. He told the waters to separate. He spoke light into being. Isn't that amazing? Also, consider that when He created light and separated it from darkness, that began the first measurement of time.

So, God created the light and said it was good. This means He was satisfied with His creation.

Following the separations of the waters, He created the first garden before He created the sun, the moon, stars, or even humans. God created the garden for His enjoyment with the humans He breathed life into humans. He loves to garden and watch it grow and prosper.

He created all things to recreate and populate on their own. Think about how He created animals, plants, birds, sea mammals, etc. Most all of them can procreate on their own. God actually created the plants for all of the other creatures to eat.

He created the plants to bring life to His other creations. We receive our oxygen from trees, medicine, and many other sources.

It is so amazing how God provided for us through this creation.

Genesis 1:11-12

11 And God said, Let the earth bring forth grass, the herb yielding seed, and the fruit tree yielding fruit after his kind, whose seed is in itself, upon the earth: and it was so.

12 And the earth brought forth grass, and herb yielding seed after his kind, and the tree yielding fruit, whose seed was in itself, after his kind: and God saw that it was good.

Notice how God said, "Let the Earth bring forth grass" upon itself. He then proclaimed that fruit trees would yield fruit after their kind. He gave the fruit trees seed within themselves to create other fruit trees. Isn't that awesome that God gave the Earth the power to create within itself?

Genesis 1:29-30

29 And God said, Behold, I have given you every herb bearing seed, which is upon the face of all the earth, and every tree, in the which is the fruit of a tree yielding seed; to you it shall be for meat.

30 And to every beast of the earth, and to every fowl of the air, and to everything that creepeth upon the earth, wherein there is life, I have given every green herb for meat: and it was so.

A fruit encases a seed within itself to reproduce.

According to Dictionary.com;

Fruit [froot]

noun, plural fruits (especially collectively) fruit.

1. any product of plant growth useful to humans or animals.

2. the developed ovary of a seed plant with its contents and accessory parts, as the pea pod, nut, tomato, or pineapple.

3. the edible part of a plant developed from a flower, with any accessory tissues, as the peach, mulberry, or banana.

4. the spores and accessory organs of ferns, mosses, fungi, algae, or lichen.

5. anything produced or accruing; product, result, or effect; return or profit: the fruits of one's labors.

6. Slang: Extremely Disparaging and Offensive. a contemptuous term used to refer to a male homosexual.

verb (used with or without object)

7. to bear or cause to bear fruit: a tree that fruits in late summer; careful pruning that sometimes fruits a tree. (Dictionary.com, 2016)

An interesting fact is that the pine tree creates pine cones and which are considered in the fruit category because they encase seeds. These seeds are often called nuts. Though the seeds, or nuts, are edible, they are tiny and afford little value as a food to humans. They have wings too! According to Survival-Manual.com "You will recognize the seeds because they look sort of like an insect wing. One wing with a bump at the base. The bump is the nut... the pine seed. The wind is used as a means for the seed to catch a breeze and be spread far from the parent tree." (Survivor-Manual.com, ND)

See how God was pleased with His creation? He created, spoke, then sat back and admired His work. Imagine how much time it took for Him to be very specific about each piece. Why did He make one tree look like it does and have certain characteristics different from other trees? He took a lot of time to make each creation different.

According to Better Homes and Gardens

There are 18 different types of fruit:

Apple | Blackberry | Blueberry | Fig | Fuchsia | Flowering Gooseberry | Grape | Lemon | Lime | Loquat| Nectarine | Orange | Pawpaw | Peach Pear Plum Raspberry Strawberry Sweet Cherry (tart, pie and bing as well) **Note – Tomatoes & Cucumbers are fruits too! They bear seeds**

God Likes Variety!

On the first day, God created the heavens and the Earth. He created the light of day and night. On the second day, He created the heavens. He created the expanse between the midst of the waters.

26

He separated the waters and commanded c
which He called Earth.

He created the garden on the third day. Ho
garden for Him to create it on the third day? F
night and day lights, and then the creatures of
birds of the air. He commanded even those birds and creatures to
be fruitful and multiply.

Genesis 2:4-5

4 These are the generations of the heavens and of the earth when they were created, in the day that the Lord God made the earth and the heavens,

5 And every plant of the field before it was in the earth, and every herb of the field before it grew: for the Lord God had not caused it to rain upon the earth, and there was not a man to till the ground.

It is interesting to note the above-referenced scriptures. Did you notice how God created the plants and herbs before he put them in the Earth? This is how much He loved His creation. He waited to put them in the Earth until man could take care of them. He must have supernaturally taken care of those plants. It is kind of how He does us today in the spirit. Our roots attach to the heavenly vines and rivers. I imagine it was the same way for the first plants and herbs. See how awesome God is with His creation?

Following that first part of creation, He created every living creeping thing, creatures and beasts and livestock on the Earth. Then God created man to have dominion over the whole garden. He created man in His image. He told the man:

...d enjoyed His garden so much that He could walk through it ...the cool of the day and talk to His creation. He designed us to look like Him, and He even gave us dominion over all the Earth. We had it made!

> *Genesis 1:26 - And God said, Let us make man in our image, after our likeness: and let them have dominion over the fish of the sea, and over the fowl of the air, and over the cattle, and over all the earth, and over every creeping thing that creepeth upon the earth.*

Can you imagine a God who loved humanity so much that He would leave Heaven and come down to Earth to walk around enjoying His creation? He took the time and effort to build a personal relationship with His creation. I can see God just walking and admiring the peach trees, the apple trees, etc. God probably talked to the trees and animals too. When He created each day and saw that it was good, God wanted to feel satisfied with His creation.

So, walking around the garden probably brought a tremendous amount of satisfaction to God.

Can you imagine the purity of their relationship at this point? Here, Adam and Eve have easy access to food. They could talk to the animals, watch fish swim and birds fly? It had to be amazing just to be that free.

They walked around the garden not fearing anything. Everything was at their beck and call. God gave them dominion over everything. They were protected by God and did not have any idea of what evil meant. It must have been somewhat like being in a glass house or a bubble. This garden was a very special place.

When they were walking in obedience to God and not sinning by eating of the wrong tree, they were in this garden of protection. They had a relationship with God and had dominion over the whole Earth. Everything was readily accessible to them. They did not have to work for any provision. They just strictly had to obey God, and all things were provided.

This is how God wants our relationship to be with Him. He desires that it be like what He had with Adam and Eve in the original garden, His Garden of Eden. He wants us naked in the spirit and transparent with Him. He wants us laying it all out there and being transparent before Him. This is the reason God loved David so much. Although David did stupid things, he kept his heart right before God. He was quick to repent and answer to God for his life.

He was transparent before God, and according to 1 Samuel 13:14, He sought out David as a man after His own heart.

Have you have turned your back on God? If you have, you would have known that the dome (the protection over us which I call a dome) had been lifted. You realized that you had no protection, and you were out there for the wolves.

I could feel His protection has gone. Also, when I saw things happen to my family, I knew I couldn't do anything about it because I had no standing with God. I was powerless over any situation because of my choice to be on my own without God.

The dome is a serious thing and a blessing to us when we are in obedience. When we are walking in obedience, we are walking in that secret garden all the time. We are walking in that dome of a secret place. We are in a dome of light. It is a dome of His glory, protection, love, and shield.

One time, I was walking in a back alley in Nashville, and two men were approaching me. I sensed that they wanted to harm me

When they were close to me, I said, "No! In the name of Jesus!" It frightened them, and they ran away.

I can think of many times that this dome has protected me. One time, I hosted a prayer meeting with about twelve other ladies from the community. I told them I saw angels in the room as tall as the building with big swords with flames of fire on them. Next thing you know, a family member slams the door open and started cussing me out. She did not like me taking her daughter to a Pentecostal church and was mad I had this prayer meeting in her daughter's house. After cussing me out and telling me that she demanded I stay away from her daughter, she walked over to me and threw her arm back to swing and punch me in the nose. She got about five inches from my nose and the angels held her fist back! Her fisted dangled there shaking fighting against this force. Suddenly her eyes became big as saucers and she became so scared that she ran out of the room! The ladies at the prayer meeting were so shocked.

Time and time again, God's protection has been over me. It is also over you when you are living in obedience to our Creator! I must say as well that when I was not right with God,

I knew I was open game to the wolves. I could feel that the protection had been lifted. It is much better to stay under His wing of protection.

Talking about protection, I had to include Psalm 91!

Psalm 91:1-16

1 He that dwelleth in the secret place of the most High shall abide under the shadow of the Almighty.

---

2 I will say of the Lord, He is my refuge and my fortress: my God; in him will I trust.

3 Surely he shall deliver thee from the snare of the fowler, and from the noisome pestilence.

4 He shall cover thee with his feathers, and under his wings shalt thou trust: his truth shall be thy shield and buckler.

5 Thou shalt not be afraid for the terror by night; nor for the arrow that flieth by day;

6 Nor for the pestilence that walketh in darkness; nor for the destruction that wasteth at noonday.

7 A thousand shall fall at thy side, and ten thousand at thy right hand; but it shall not come nigh thee.

8 Only with thine eyes shalt thou behold and see the reward of the wicked.

9 Because thou hast made the Lord, which is my refuge, even the most High, thy habitation;

10 There shall no evil befall thee, neither shall any plague come nigh thy dwelling.

11 For he shall give his angels charge over thee, to keep thee in all thy ways.

12 They shall bear thee up in their hands, lest thou dash thy foot against a stone.

13 Thou shalt tread upon the lion and adder: the young lion and the dragon shalt thou trample under feet.

14 Because he hath set his love upon me, therefore will I deliver him: I will set him on high, because he hath known my name.

15 He shall call upon me, and I will answer him: I will be with him in trouble; I will deliver him, and honour him.

16 With long life will I satisfy him, and shew him my salvation.

Oh how wonderful it is to be under His wing. Do you know how mighty those wings must be? Think about it a minute. I imagine a big white wing with very strong muscles and beautiful feathers that are translucent! I see a wing that grasps every part of my being and snuggles it! I see a wing that embraces me with no area exposed!

I feel the warmth, love, compassion, safety, and a shield of gold on the outside of the wing! I see the tips of the wings like tender fingers brushing my brows. Oh how majestic is His name and how mighty just the embrace of our Father! We are blessed Bride!

Supernatural Garden

I declare that when we are obedient to God, we walk in the supernatural garden at all times. This is how we can pray to God even while we're talking to other people. This is how we immediately enter into His presence when we begin praying out loud or worshipping. We walk in a continual state of prayer, fellowship, and communion with God.

When we are in obedience, we are walking in a glory realm called the Garden.

I also declare that the Garden of Eden is a physical representation of the spiritual. I believe God gives us trees on Earth to help us live and to be a visual to our spirit man. For example, God gave man a seed (sperm) to impart into a woman (another type of soil). The seed then enters into the womb of protection (underground). The mother (host) cultivates that seed, and it is supernaturally connected to the vine (umbilical cord). .

Our supernatural garden must be cultivated, attended to and maintained on a daily basis. We must not neglect this garden or our seeds will die. God downloads or implants seeds into us that will require faith to cultivate and germinate that seed. He desires us to bring this thing from Heaven to life! Yes, it will be a process and challenging, but God will bless you for bringing Heaven to Earth!

Prayer cultivates the seeds. Prayer makes it grow and gives it strength. The presence of our savior is what gives the seed sunlight. It causes it to be illuminated and it responds.

I delve into more of this in the rest of the book...

3

THE ULTIMATE GARDENER

A gardener is a caretaker of a garden. That's pretty simple. This is the official definition of a gardener:

Gardener – noun -a person who is employed to cultivate or care for a garden, lawn, etc. Or, any person who gardens or is skillful in gardening. (Random House Dictionary, 2016)

They care about the plants, people, animals, etc. Gardeners are responsible for cultivating, pruning, protecting, and ensuring healthy growth. In our case, God the Father is the Ultimate Gardener and the Holy Spirit is the Caretaker. The Holy Spirit makes sure the garden is pruned, in shape, focused, etc.

The Creator as Ultimate Gardener

The Ultimate Gardener has a plan for every tree in His garden. Our trees do not have a choice as to where they're planted, but we DO have a choice as to whether or not we allow the author and finisher of our faith to FINISH THAT TREE STORY. Do we allow our trees to grow up bitter and sad? Do we think we can make better decisions than our Gardener? Or, do we let our tree grow to the One who created it, and let Him make the fruit on that tree? Our creator knows exactly what He is doing with our garden if we will just trust Him to do it.

John 15:1-17

1 I am the true vine, and my Father is the husbandman [Gardener in other versions].

2 Every branch in me that beareth not fruit he taketh away: and every branch that beareth fruit, he purgeth it, that it may bring forth more fruit.

3 Now ye are clean through the word which I have spoken unto you.

4 Abide in me, and I in you. As the branch cannot bear fruit of itself, except it abide in the vine; no more can ye, except ye abide in me.

5 I am the vine, ye are the branches: He that abideth in me, and I in him, the same bringeth forth much fruit: for without me ye can do nothing.

6 If a man abide not in me, he is cast forth as a branch, and is withered; and men gather them, and cast them into the fire, and they are burned.

7 If ye abide in me, and my words abide in you, ye shall ask what ye will, and it shall be done unto you.

8 Herein is my Father glorified, that ye bear much fruit; so shall ye be my disciples.

9 As the Father hath loved me, so have I loved you: continue ye in my love.

10 If ye keep my commandments, ye shall abide in my love; even as I have kept my Father's commandments, and abide in his love.

11 These things have I spoken unto you, that my joy might remain in you, and that your joy might be full.

12 This is my commandment, That ye love one another, as I have loved you.

13 Greater love hath no man than this, that a man lay down his life for his friends.

14 Ye are my friends, if ye do whatsoever I command you.

15 Henceforth I call you not servants; for the servant knoweth not what his lord doeth: but I have called you friends; for all things that I have heard of my Father I have made known unto you.

16 Ye have not chosen me, but I have chosen you, and ordained you, that ye should go and bring forth fruit, and that your fruit should remain: that whatsoever ye shall ask of the Father in my name, he may give it you.

17 These things I command you, that ye love one another.

The Ultimate Gardener created His garden to bear much fruit. He specifically designed the garden to protect, supply, communicate, and enjoy with His creation. As I stated earlier, the whole garden is symbolic of our spiritual experience with God.

Leaves Blowing Away From Your Tree

I've interviewed pastors and ministers for the past couple of years and have learned a lot! Pastors have talked about how some pastors are led by fear because they're afraid they'll offend people and lose church members.

They are also afraid that the leaves from their trees will blow off to another tree, and they'll lose their offerings and other benefits from those particular leaves that were previously attached to them.

Let me clarify that we are held accountable to God for how we produce fruit. We are not held accountable for how the leaves or branches handle that fruit. If they decide to fly away and attach to another tree, then we must release them. We obey God. Period! They are not and were never your life source. God, the Ultimate Gardener, is the source. Obeying God is where your wealth is!

So many times pastors have changed their whole ministries because of this. They have quit preaching sin....Hellfire and brimstone....and speaking truth! I'm not saying we must preach in this style, but preaching truth is a must.

They are too busy growing their churches through self-help sermons or as I like to call it, self-help gurus! Pastors, your flock can get that through a psychologist! Let the world do that for them. You follow the Holy Ghost, who is the Caretaker of God's garden. Let Him lead you on what to preach and how to run your ministries!

Gardener Knows What He Is Doing

Did you know that a tree has no choice as to where it's planted? Did you know that some trees are in very violent circumstances?

38

Maybe they're in very dry places. Maybe they're in flooded areas. Maybe they're in constant storms and hurricanes!

Did you know that some trees have missing limbs or missing bark? We have fat trees, skinny trees, tall trees, **and** short trees. We have beautiful trees, ugly trees, and trees of all different colors with many different manifestations! However, they are all God's trees!

Example: God wrote Johnny Joe's book before Johnny Joe came to Earth. Johnny Joe was raised in a very violent home. He was constantly told that he wasn't worth anything. Daddy drank and was an alcoholic. Momma cheated on daddy all the time because daddy was so mean to her. Uncle Joe constantly smacked Johnny Joe around. Because Johnny Joe was not raised in church to hear how God loves him, He became bitter. **He** started abusing animals due to the pain that was inside his tree. His tree became cold, calloused, and hard.

Years later, Johnny Joe met a girl and fell in love. His heart became softer, and he started letting down his bark to become able to love. Johnny Joe's wife got saved, and her tree changed! All of a sudden, her tree stopped being angry. **It** quit cursing and doing all the crazy things it had been doing because it was sad inside.

Well, ole Johnny Joe saw the changes and went to church with his wife to see what all the fuss was about.

After watching and learning, Johnny Joe went to a prayer meeting one night and released his tree to the Ultimate Gardener. The Ultimate Gardener had been waiting for the day when Johnny Joe would reach out to Him so that He could show him the REAL destiny He had for him.

The Ultimate Gardener wanted to make a mighty army out of this sad oak tree. He wanted to make His little plants mighty warriors!

The Ultimate Gardener had this book pre-written for Johnny Joe if Johnny Joe would only release his tree.

So Johnny Joe surrenders to the Ultimate Gardener at this meeting, and he has a LIFE-changing moment. All the hardness, blackness, and evil were released out of his tree.

So, Johnny Joe embraced his wife and repents for all the years of evil he had poured upon her tree, and they forgave one another. Then, the parent trees came together and rebuked the devourer off their little plants.

Until the next day!

The next day, Johnny Joe went to work. He was shocked to discover that his tree was now bare before the whole other evil garden! They all saw that his tree was different and that he was beautiful and saved. So, they persecuted and made fun of this new tree! They didn't like how it had changed. They wanted the old tree back!

Since Johnny Joe had dealt with rejection since he was a little boy, **he** couldn't take it. He went home and informed his beautiful wife that he was not doing that anymore.

He rejected the Ultimate Gardener and turned his back on him, because he was more comfortable in his old tree skin.

So, he became meaner to his wife over the years and even threatened to kill her and the little plants many times. The Ultimate Gardener ended up separating the two trees so that the one tree could raise the three little plants according to the Ultimate Gardener's plan. It was hard on the momma tree, but she did it. Now, the little plants are full grown trees searching for their destinies with the Ultimate Gardener.

Now, what would have happened to those little plants if they had stayed in that violent situation? Their tree stories may have been different.

Their trees may have ended up like Johnny Joe's heart.

You ask what happened to Johnny Joe. Well, he ended up marrying a couple more times, and he has now been happily married to a woman for over ten years. We pray for Johnny Joe to surrender to his Creator so that he can discover the true plan for his life!

His Trees Have a Will and Choice in the Garden

Well now that you get the picture of God and his garden...this is what He told me when He woke me up the other morning...

Did you know that if that tree is stubborn and rebellious to the gardener that He will pluck that tree up and throw him in the fire because it's dead and not producing any fruit!

He loves ALL THE TREES and HOPES they all make the right decision to trust Him and allow Him to prune it, shape it, clean it, wash it, fill it, decorate it, restore it, shine it, and maybe even replant that tree to where it can bear much more fruit! He is the ultimate gardener and we trust God with that tree! All we have to do is keep our roots planted firmly in Jesus!

He is jealous for you!

4

GOD & RELATIONSHIP TO MAN

When God created the Garden of Eden, He placed Adam in it to take care of His creation. He had a specific reason for that garden. It was in that garden that He created Eve as a helpmate for Adam. The garden was originally created to be a tabernacle for relationship between God and man.

The Relationship Begins

God enjoyed walking around and talking to Adam and Eve. I can just God walking around in the Garden and admiring the fruit trees. I can imagine Him picking a peach and enjoying His creation. I picture Him playing hide and seek with Adam and just having fun. He created man in His image.

As God had this conversation with the rest of the Trinity, (Jesus the Son, Holy Spirit as the teacher and guide, and God the Father), He said, "Hey, while we're creating everything, let's create a man with whom we can have a relationship. Let's see if he will choose to love, serve, and be with Us. We want him to have a will and make a choice to be pure or to be self-centered (pride). This will prevent another Lucifer incident in Heaven."

Lucifer was the chief angel and got kicked out of Heaven because of pride. He rose up against God and took almost 1/3 of the angels with him.

He thought he was just as important as God and tried to form a revolt against God.

God Became Daddy God & Protector

Just as parents want to protect their children from all the evil in the world, God wants to protect us. God instructed Adam and Eve not to eat of the Tree of Knowledge of Good and Evil. He wanted to keep His creation pure, only knowing good, healthy things. It's somewhat like our children. Would you want to tell your five year old child or grandchild, who sits on your lap and has so much love and innocence, about how other children their age are being beaten, molested, raped, tortured, etc.? NO! Just because you have the knowledge of the evil in the world does not mean you want your children to gain knowledge of it.

Malachi 2:10 Have we not all one father? hath not one God created us? why do we deal treacherously every man against his brother, by profaning the covenant of our fathers?

I must insert a story here. I was at a community gathering for adults. One family brought their 10 year-old son to wait while they rehearsed. He had his tablet and was occupied. I happen to glance at the screen and saw a person's head literally being blown to smithereens. It displayed all the gore, etc. I was horrified! It made my heart sink!

I'm not used to violence anymore. This boy did not flinch. I walked up to him and said, "Is this a video game?" He said, "No that was just a video that popped up." I replied, "Yes, but I saw a head being blown up." He replied, "Yes, I know," and laughed. His parents were not watching what he was being fed by this tablet.

44

He obviously was not bothered by the horror scene. This is sad.

So, God wanted to protect his children and to keep their roots clean. When Adam and Eve sinned, their conscience was awakened to their actions, and they covered their nakedness.

No longer were they transparent and holy before God. They felt dirty and had to cover their sin. Never before had they known shame, guilt, or evil. Once they partook of the Tree of Knowledge, their trees, their temples of the Holy Spirit, were tainted.

Once this happened, it severed their relationship with God because God cannot dwell with sin. He had to cast them out of the garden, having mercy on them enough to clothe and protect them. God performed the first sacrifice to cover their sins. He killed an animal to clothe his beloved Adam and Eve.

> *Genesis 3:21- "Unto Adam also and to his wife did the Lord God make coats of skin and clothed them."*

Although He had to punish them and cast them out of the garden that He had created for them, He still had mercy and covered them with skins, providing protection from the elements such as the bushes in the forests, etc. The skins served many purposes I'm sure.

> *Genesis 3:21 - Unto Adam also and to his wife did the Lord God make coats of skins, and clothed them.*

DIFFERENCES IN COMMUNICATION BETWEEN TREES & MAN TO GOD

When God created the trees and plants, He made them living beings. Plants have cells just like we do.

It's very fascinating to study the cells of plants because they are like a total planetary system within. Have you ever wondered how the trees carry water from the roots all the way up to the tops of the tall trees?

It's amazing how God created all the cells to work together to bring life to trees and plants. The Bible mentions that the trees even clap their hands and praise God.

> *Isaiah 55:12 -The trees of the fields shall clap their hands.*

> *Psalm 98:8 – Let the floods clap their hands and let the hills be joyful together*

Obviously God's creation praises Him at all times. There are many scriptures about the rocks crying out and the birds singing to Him, etc., but they only communicate with Him. Sometimes, He talks back to them as well, but it's not the same type of communication we have with God.

We have boldness through Jesus to go into the Holy of Holies and have communion with God. We have access to a relationship with Him. He created us to worship Him and to have a relationship with Him.

Why would He need humans if He only wanted us to praise Him and not have a relationship? He has His creation to do that. They all praise Him. He wants more than that from us. He wants us to get to know Him.

46

Think of the many times God has carried on with debates with humans He created. One that comes to mind is Abraham.

When God told him that He was destroying Sodom and Gomorrah, Abraham asked Him many times to reconsider. It caused God to consider saving Sodom and Gomorrah.

There are several instances where man has changed God's mind. Even in the case of Abraham, God said, "Should we confide in Abraham our plans?"

Genesis 18:16 -23

16 And the men rose up from thence, and looked toward Sodom: and Abraham went with them to bring them on the way.

17 And the Lord said, Shall I hide from Abraham that thing which I do;

18 Seeing that Abraham shall surely become a great and mighty nation, and all the nations of the earth shall be blessed in him?

19 For I know him, that he will command his children and his household after him, and they shall keep the way of the Lord, to do justice and judgment; that the Lord may bring upon Abraham that which he hath spoken of him.

20 And the Lord said, Because the cry of Sodom and Gomorrah is great, and because their sin is very grievous;

21 I will go down now, and see whether they have done altogether according to the cry of it, which is come unto me; and if not, I will know.

22 And the men turned their faces from thence, and went toward Sodom: but Abraham stood yet before the Lord.

23 And Abraham drew near, and said, Wilt thou also destroy the righteous with the wicked?

So, He wants to build a relationship with us as our loving, caring, protecting Father God.

In the Old Testament, one was only allowed to go through priests and God's prophets unless God had a specific purpose for him. The people met once a year and gave sacrifices to the priests for them to sacrifice to God for their sins. It was not for forgiveness but was for just a covering of their sins. The priest would place the blood of the sacrifices on escape goats, lay hands on them, imparting the sins of the people onto those goats, and they would then send them off to dry places.

FYI: This process is a reflection of humanity. Christians are symbolized as sheep because we follow and obey God. Sinners are likened unto goats because they are rebellious to God and represent demons. Many times when people are casting demons out, they send them out to the deep, dark, dry places never to return again. The goat is the satanic church's symbol and represents rebellion towards God. They call him Baphomet. Research this demon and how society worships him. It's sad.

So, God desires to have a relationship with His creation. In the Old Testament, it came through the sacrifice of innocent animals and the pure blood to cover the sins of God's people.

48

God sent His only begotten Son, Jesus Christ, Yeshua, Messiah, to be the ultimate sacrifice and perfect Lamb. It opened up the door wide for us to be able to communicate with God intimately.

Now that we have that open door to the throne room, we can enter in boldly and talk to Daddy God about our lives or anything else we want. It totally changed humanity.

God to the Trees & Humanity

God desires for His people to sit quiet and listen to His voice. He talks to us in many different ways. When we walk in obedience, we can know His voice more clearly.

Here are the many ways God can talk to you:

Through Trials, Tribulations, & Circumstances

Just like trees in His garden, He knows how to get our attention. One great example of this is one of my spiritual fathers. This is all public now so I can mention this in the book. In July of 2015, he hosted a big meeting. He hosts this conference at his church and he opens the first night with a powerful prophetic word for the people in attendance and those watching online.

At the conference in 2015, something very unusual happened. He approached the platform and repented to the church because God had rebuked him for not raising up sons and daughters and allowing others to use that platform. In other words he was not sharing the platform. After his repentance, he opened up his platform for a minister from South Africa. He surrendered his pulpit back to God.

It was later revealed that he had cancer of the throat. He went through chemotherapy and the whole process.

During this time God did an amazing thing. Ministers from all over the world came and ministered FOR FREE!

They did not even charge him, but showed him love for his life and ministry.

Since that time, he has opened his pulpit to God's sons and daughters.

He listened to the winds of change. When circumstances hit him and were out of control, he got on his face before a Holy God and asked Him why this door was opened. God answered his request, and it changed his whole life and ministry.

So, anytime something happens in your life, instead of blaming others, rebuking the devil, or getting angry about it, get on your face before your Creator and ask Him if you opened a door somewhere to the enemy, and repent.

He will allow circumstances to get your attention! Pastor Anthony Daley in Clarksville, Tennessee at The Tabernacle Church said, "If you are in a situation and you are wondering why God allowed it to happen, then think about it like this: If you are in a storm and you did not do anything to cause it, then it's God trying to change other people. If you're in the storm and you caused it through disobedience, then God is trying to change you." This was profound! I heard him preach this when I attended his church at the beginning of my pit (fiery trial and suffering). This let me know that God was throwing me in the PIT to change other people and me. People are watching and waiting to see what God is going to do with my life.

We are always books read by men. I have been in this PIT for three years, but I know I am coming out now. I'm writing this book in my PIT.

I'm in a little trailer in the country with horses, chickens, a pond, and a sheep dog. We call this trailer, "Little Cabin on the Hill". We say this because God always provides a cabin for me to write books. It's really amazing.

God has supernaturally provided for me in the three years. During this time, God has helped me to write four books.

The whole point is for us to get on our face before the Ultimate Creator and say, "Okay daddy, this is happening in my life. Please search my heart, and let me know if I opened a door somehow to the enemy. What it is that you're trying to tell me? I am listening. You have my attention."

We are humbling ourselves before a holy, just, and powerful God who created the whole entire universe. He's the God who is the Great I AM! He is Jehovah God! Who are we to question His decisions? We know that when things happen in our lives, God gave His permission. Think of how He did with Job. Satan came to God and wanted to sift Job. God granted permission; however, He told Satan that he could not kill Job. God knows what He is doing. We must trust Him in the process, and wait upon Him.

When preachers proclaim that God does not allow suffering and it is all attacks from the devil, it dismisses accountability to our Creator. It takes away from self-examination and humbling before our God and King. We know that Satan crouches at the door to come in, but he can't unless we open a door. He's like a policeman. He's waiting for us to break the law.

Yes, I do believe we still take the word of God and claim it over our lives, etc.; however, we must still humble ourselves and go before God about our trials and tribulations. We may be surprised at what God says. He may just reveal something.

God Speaks Through His Word
2 Timothy 3:16, Psalm 119:11, 105

God talks to us through His Word, the Bible. The Bible says that as we read it, **it** cuts us like a knife to the marrow and bone. It says that it is the searcher of man's hearts.

His Word is basically seeds that are supernaturally planted within us as we read through the eye-gate. Or, if we listen to the Bible, it is depositing seeds in our ear-gate. If we read the Bible as we are watching it through our eye-gate and speaking it out of our mouth-gate, then we are capturing all three gates, the eye-gate, the ear-gate, and the mouth-gate. This is the best way to read it.

Studying the Bible is also a way to cut through the lies that the enemy tries to get us to believe. When we read His Word, truth is imparted into us and reveals the lies that are inside our tree.

As we receive or allow the seeds of doubt, unbelief, or lies into our tree, the Word of God is receiving in the supernatural the seeds from the Tree of Life in Heaven.

This tree is more powerful than any of those seeds within our tree. This tree's seeds come in our tree and EXPOSE the enemy that has moved in unaware. This is why we must read the Word of God, and be sober and alert. Here are a few scriptures about how God talks to us through His word:

God Speaks Through the Holy Spirit
Acts 11:12, Acts 13:2, Acts 16:6-7, 1 Kings 19:12,
Isaiah 30:19-21

God talks to us through the Holy Spirit. He indwells us as a guide and teacher. He works with our conscience to guide us in right and wrong. When we feel that nudge on the inside or a feeling that doesn't sit right about something, that is the Holy Spirit warning us. I could write a whole book on how the Holy Spirit talks to us, but just pray and ask Him to talk to you and allow you to clearly hear Him. I will say this for myself, He always warns me before something bad happens. He always keeps me informed so that I can handle it better. Please trust Him as your superpower friend.

God Speaks Through Other People
Proverbs 12:15

God will speak to you through other people. This is especially true when He's confirming something to you through other people. I'll give you one example.

I was in Bible College when God woke me one morning at 4:00 a.m. and said, "Because you gave up your house and car for me, I'm going to bless you with a better house than you could ever dream of and a brand new car!"

So I was very thankful. That night at the Winter Formal, I went out to eat with about 12 other Bible College students. I was telling them about what God had said to me that morning. They all knew the struggle I had had and how I had lost everything to follow Him. They were shocked when a man walked in the restaurant, stopped what he was doing, and said, "Thus sayeth the Lord. Because you gave up your house and car for me, I'm about to bless you with a better house than you could ever dream of and a brand new car!" He yelled this across the restaurant as he was pointing his finger at me.

Everyone sitting at the table had their mouths to the floor! They were so shocked! I said, "I told you!" Then, we all laughed.

The point is that things like that demonstrate how the Holy Spirit talks to us. Other times, it's in prophetic words, encouragement, etc. Sometimes, it is to rebuke us or chastise us.

The key to someone else speaking critically into our lives is that we must be like Moses and not get upset at their criticism or rebuke. Instead, we must go back to God with it and say, "Are they telling me the truth, God? Is there something about me that I'm not seeing? Show me my heart, oh God!" Then, we are not only humbling ourselves before God and that person, but we are walking in meekness.

Meekness says that although I don't understand what you're saying, I will pray about it and ask God to show me if it is true.

So don't be so quick to dismiss them if it is in line with the Word of God. If they are just being mean and calling you names or whatever, then you cast those far from you.

God Speaks Through Dreams & Visions
Matthew 1:20-21, Acts 10:9-18

I could write another book on this one as well. I have experienced dreams and visions from God since I was a little girl.

I know when they are His dreams and when it's the enemy. However, God speaks to me most of the time in dreams. He will give me strategic dreams where He will say, "Get up and go do this. Call this person. Do this or do that." It's pretty amazing and many times when I'm really confused about something, I will ask Him to give me a dream and make it clear. He always does!

God Speaks Audible
Acts 9:4 -5

I heard God's audible voice one time. I wrote about this experience in my first book. I was taking some youth to an event in another town and He spoke in the car and called my name. Thankfully He allowed one other girl to hear it too so they wouldn't think I was crazy. Yes, He will talk to you audibly sometimes. Many people on Earth have heard His voice audible!

God Speaks Through Angels
Luke 1:26-38

God spoke to Mary through an angel and many other people in the Bible. He can speak to His Bride today through angels.

God Speaks Through Anything/Nature
Numbers 22:28

God can speak through anything. We know He talked through a donkey one time. This is my most favorite story in the Bible. I laugh so hard thinking about how Balaam kept beating the donkey because the donkey wouldn't mind him.

Then the donkey turned around and said, "Would you stop beating me already?" (My interpretation). God can talk to us through nature, animals, birds, and anything He wants!

The key is if we are paying attention to hear Him. It can be in the simple things. There are horses here where I'm staying. Today we had a thunderstorm as I'm writing this book. I happen to look outside and the horses were standing on the edge of the pond looking so beautiful. It was pouring down road and very big drops.

They were still eating the grass until a loud roar of thunder shook the ground and lasted a good 30 seconds or so. The most amazing thing happened. The horses froze in position while it was thundering and did not move until it was over. All I could think was how they were thinking, "OK Master Creator, we hear you." It is like every creation will bow to the name of Jesus! When God speaks they all listen. See, this is another way God speaks to us. God let me know that He has a relationship with all living things. It's really amazing.

I'll share another story. My mother was sick and recently released from the hospital. She has COPD (this is fact, but not truth), and she was laying on her bed with a breathing mask and could hardly breath. I held her hand as I looked out the window and screamed at the devil! I told him to leave my mother alone and to back off! I was praying and asking God to have mercy on mom and heal her, etc. So, I look out the window and there is the prettiest red bird.

Well, the 'ole red bird kept coming to the window and visiting her while she was sick and wearing oxygen. She would tell me how the red bird came to visit her.

See, this was God talking to me and mom. He sent that red bird to comfort my mother. It's the simple things if we will open our eyes to see.

Now that I live out of state, sometimes I'll ask mom if she has seen the red bird... She will say, "No, I'm hardly in my room anymore." This lets me know my mother is doing well. She no longer needs that little red bird. God is so good!

5

THE TREE OF KNOWLEDGE

What Is This Tree?

In the Garden of Eden God placed two very significant trees in the middle. One is the Tree of Life, which breeds life eternal. The other tree brings death, which is the Tree of Knowledge of Good and Evil. Adam and Eve were forbidden to touch that tree. God told Adam that the moment they ate of that tree, they would surely die. Of course, God meant spiritually.

When they ate of the wrong tree (the Tree of Knowledge which represents the carnal spirit), their spirit man died. They were still living (like dead-man walking), but the spirit-man that God had breathed into them died. Once Adam and Eve ate of the beautiful, rotten fruit of that tree, it tainted their trees and implanted a virus. God could no longer have open communication with them or be around them, as He had enjoyed before.

Satan twisted God's words to entice them to eat the fruit. He said, "You shall not surely die." He lured Eve based on her carnal lust. It was basically pride that caught her in the trap of the spider's web. Lust says, "How will this benefit me?" It attracts a me, me, me spirit. The Tree of Knowledge of Good and Evil is built for the carnal nature and to impart things to build their "me" up. Look at the words in the tree:

Once Satan convinced humanity to partake of the forbidden fruit, it gave him the full rights to the earthly realm, which they were stewards of.

He bought the kingdom once he conned and convinced the royalty couple that they could partake of this sin.

Once he had full rights to the earthly realm, he began the terror plot. He convinced Cain to kill Abel, and there are many other

Tree of Knowledge of Good & Evil

ways by which he influenced the people of the Old Testament.

Is This Tree Still Here?

I want to tell you about how this Tree of Knowledge operates in today's society. It's not an actual tree, but it is still participating with the god of the world and the ungodly world system.

We only have one life to live on Earth. God created our destiny path for His purpose before time began. He already knew us before we were manifested on Earth.

He has a destiny pre-written and designed for each of us, if we will surrender our trees totally to Him. He wants each person to reveal to humanity another aspect of who God is. We are all here to bring another revelation of Him.

Some people can live through unfathomable experiences, anguish, and pain because they were called to overcome that specific thing to glorify and give thanks to God in and through it all. It's not that God is being meaner to this family than to another, but it's a result of our forefathers' relationships with God. We may still be dealing with some of their generational sins and spiritual roots they passed down or some of their blessings, too. In either case, we are designed to show humanity how God can help with that certain area, etc.

How Do We Eat From This Tree Today?

In today's culture, we participate in the Tree of Knowledge through the worldly gateways such as television, radio, advertisings, government, the public sector, state-run educational systems, etc. Almost everything in popular culture is opposite of God's world (the Christian world).

By filling our temples of the Holy Spirit with the ungodly data and information from worldly impartations by the antichrist spirit of television, movies, music, books, radio, advertisements, entertainment, social gatherings, etc., we are eating the wrong food or fruit. It poisons our temples and hardens our roots so that we cannot receive from the rivers of living water.

Remember the following old adages that are still true today:

- "Trash in, trash out."

Satan wanted to corrupt and pervert God's creation by conning Adam and Eve into believing it was harmless to participate in the sin (eating the fruit).

✷ Have Satan and his followers conned and lied to you lately? Remember, Satan is the "father of lies: and the truth is not in him." If Satan or his followers are speaking, they are lying. Satan is still alive and well on planet Earth.

If he can convince us that it's fine to tolerate sin in order to enjoy a good television show, then he's convinced us to eat of his fruit which brings forth death and separation from God. As already stated above, "What you eat or consume is what you are." So, if you consume the vomit that Satan is spewing out through secular and some so-called Christian shows, then it taints your temples. You are consuming Satan's evil: ideologies, sin, tolerance, intolerance, evil-thinking, etc. through the ungodly programs you are watching and supporting. The Bible says to refrain from all appearance of evil.

1 Thessalonians 5:22 – Abstain from all appearance of evil. (KJV)

Will This Tree Affect My Roots?

You know the old saying, "Give the devil an inch, and he will take a mile." It's so true. If you compromise the fruit you eat, you may end up consuming the whole tree. He does not play around and neither should we.

Many people say they will not take the mark of the beast, because they know they will go to Hell if they do. However, if they eat enough of the ungodly, satanic fruit of the Knowledge of Good and Evil Tree, they may no longer be able to tell the difference between the godly and the ungodly.

They may let their defenses down, and when the pressures are on, they may willingly accept it.

> ***Matthew 15:18 – But those things which proceed out of the mouth come forth from the heart and they defile the man.***

If our tree has rotten roots, the mouth will reflect it. It will flow up through the roots to the fruit we bear as it springs forth from our mouths. Either we produce God's living water and love because we are watered and receive godly nutrients from God, or we yield Satan's contaminated water and hatred because we are watered and poisoned by him.

How does a Christian receive rotten roots? He receives them by consuming that which is evil and unhealthy within his tree. It taints the roots and clogs up the rivers of living water from flowing through their tree and producing good fruit. The Bible also says that a good tree cannot bear evil or harmful fruit. If a tree is not producing good fruit, its roots are corrupt.

The Tree of Knowledge of Good and Evil is still prevalent in our world today. Any fruits that do not reflect God's Christian world-view are tainted fruits. Think about it like this.

If new plants contaminated with a deadly virus were brought into our gardens and started infecting our good plants, we would remove and destroy those virus-laden, new plants, thus protecting the livelihood of the rest of our gardens. Sometimes God, parents, leaders, pastors, farmers, forestry personnel, doctors, etc, have to remove the bad to protect the good.

Once we see one particle of virus attach itself to another tree, we must act to remove that virus and work hard to remove the source from the garden.

We do not move it next to our tree or consume that fruit because we consider the after-effects. We remove it to protect the community. We should be careful to protect our bodies, spirits, and souls in like manner, too.

We must guard our hearts and shield them from outside interference and bad fruit-impartations through the Tree of Knowledge of Good and Evil. How do we measure what is good and what is evil? We measure it by the Word of God, the Bible, and the Holy Spirit. Sometimes the Word does not cover specifics, but the Holy Spirit is our guide and will always lead us in the right direction.

For instance, if a television program makes you feel uneasy in your heart, gut, inner man, or conscience, you are probably quenching or offending God, the Holy Spirit **that** indwells all Christians. The best thing is to just turn it off to protect yourself and not offend God who indwells you. We should all learn to listen to the nudges and the wooing of the Holy Spirit, and be quick to obey.

Proverbs 12:12 The wicked desireth the net of evil men: but the root of the righteous yieldeth fruit.

I tell children that God, the Holy Spirit, is our super power on Earth. He lives inside of us, and He will always guide us into truth. He gives us dreams, visions, talks to us, and leads us through this journey on Earth. He always knows the truth and will keep us on the right path.

Also, consider the dream I told you about with the tree in the forest and the big arrow of offense. Once that tree opened the door to the big gaping wound of offense, it allowed other arrows to stab it continually and take it out.

It ended up so cold and hard that it purposefully stepped out from under the sunshine of God's glory. At first, it knew what was holy by pushing the first arrow away, but when the big one came, it hurt right to his heart.

The tree didn't want to stop that one because it was so angry. Because he didn't forgive, it opened too many doors, and that ole tree dried up. Don't accept the fruit that Satan sends your way, no matter what form it is presented in or how good and sweet it may seem!

The Tree of Knowledge of Good and Evil Today

This evil tree is bombarding the masses today to tempt society to eat of Satan's delicious, good-looking fruit. It only satisfies briefly, and then you want more. The delicious fruit is temporary satisfactions to the flesh. Eve looked at the fruit and thought it looked delicious.

> *Genesis 3:6 - And when the woman saw that the tree was good for food, and that it was pleasant to the eyes, and a tree to be desired to make one wise, she took of the fruit thereof, and did eat, and gave also unto her husband with her; and he did eat.*

Today it is easy to see Satan's pleasant-tasting and good-looking viruses of sin intended to steal, kill and destroy if you partake of them. Some examples are pornography, drugs, illicit sex, adultery, fornication, stealing, lying, disrespect of elders, etc

John 10:10 - The thief cometh not, but for to steal, and to kill, and to destroy: I am come that they might have life, and that they might have it more abundantly

Often we are brainwashed into believing Satan and society's lies, "It is not all that bad", "You can handle it.", "Besides who will know?" You and God will know.

Later if not stopped, after Satan's poison has impacted you severely as in the case of prolonged drugs use, everyone will know.

Satan still twists God's Word today as he did in Eve's day in the Garden of Eden, convincing her that God did not really mean what He said, "You shall not surely die." Satan lied; Eve believed and was deceived, Adam sinned, and God banished them from the good life they had enjoyed. Men have been sweating in toil and women in the anguish of childbirth ever since.

The demonically inspired world culture still tries the same lies told for millennia today, "You can compromise, and it won't affect our trees." We can choose to consume the vomit that the mainstream media is flushing out through television and other forms of media. We can watch that television show with practicing homosexuals acting out on national television. We can view a thousand murder scenes a week without harm. We can watch husbands and wives cheating on each other and it not causes us to lust at our neighbor. God's answer is for His children and humanity, "No, you cannot watch sin and it not impact your life negatively and eventually brings forth spiritual and natural death!"

Think about how our churches are mixing the world system with the church. I imagine this makes God want to vomit.

I watched a ministry in Nashville play a popular Satanic Hip/Hop song on the platform! It is a song so sexual in nature. I couldn't believe it! God help us not to compromise!

I also saw another children's ministry team do a Michael Jackson dance routine to the song "Thriller" right in the front of the church on the holy platform!

God was not pleased or favorably impressed with this blatant disregard for sin in the House of the Lord at all. We must cherish God's holy sanctuary!

It is imperative that we return of the awe of God's majesty and fear of His wrath ASAP. Be careful to let no one deceive or manipulate you for their selfish purposes or hidden agendas so that we yield and serve only one supreme Master, God Almighty. We must keep all gates closed!

Too Much Knowledge Can Be Dangerous

Dr. Deven Cavalier from Revelation Ministries in Watson, Louisiana, had a profound revelation. According to her, "Adam is the one who received the word/revelation from God about not to eat of the fruit of the Knowledge of Good and Evil tree. Adam told Eve what God said, however, it was not a revelation to her because she was not granted the revelation to it. She only had head knowledge. See if people do not know the Holy Ghost and have a rhema word from God, they are going to eat of the wrong tree because they do not understand it."

She was explaining the difference between head knowledge and revelation. .

If humans seek knowledge about things without the revelation from God, it may not be from the right tree.

The Holy Spirit is there to help us understand God and his revelations.

65

Another reason the Lord desires to protect His children from the Tree of Knowledge of Good and Evil is because too much knowledge can hurt a human spirit. This is especially true from this specific tree.

By infilling this tree with this wrong type of fruit, it will clog up the roots and make the tree hard and brittle towards goodness and God.

I don't believe you can receive too much knowledge from the Tree of Life.

When we get to Heaven we will forever be reading books and learning about God. The revelations of Him will be endless. I believe we will be reading the life stories throughout eternity about each other since we are all in books. I pray your book and my book has a great ending! Oh how sad it would be for us to not finish our destiny!

6

TREE OF LIFE &
LEAVES OF HEALING

Tree of Life

In the beginning when God created the Garden, one of the trees in the middle of the Garden is the Tree of Life. This tree was special. It had the capabilities of providing life forever to the ones who ate of it. Please see this tree with all the nations represented!

Tree of Life

For as the body is one, and hath many members, and all the members of that one body, being many, are one body: so also is Christ.

Look at this:

Genesis 3: 22-24

22 And the Lord God said, Behold, the man is become as one of us, to know good and evil: and now, lest he put forth his hand, and take also of the tree of life, and eat, and live forever:

23 Therefore the Lord God sent him forth from the garden of Eden, to till the ground from whence he was taken.

24 So he drove out the man; and he placed at the east of the garden of Eden Cherubims, and a flaming sword which turned every way, to keep the way of the tree of life.

Not only did the Tree of Life contain 12 different kinds of fruit in the Book of Revelation Chapter 22, but it also contained leaves with healing for the nations.

Revelation 22:1-2

1 And he shewed me a pure river of water of life, clear as crystal, proceeding out of the throne of God and of the Lamb.

2 In the midst of the street of it, and on either side of the river, was there the tree of life, which bare twelve manner of fruits, and yielded her fruit every month: and the leaves of the tree were for the healing of the nations.

I found an article that best described the Tree of Life from a theological standpoint. This is not the whole article, but an excerpt:

The Tree Of Life
by Henry M. Morris, Ph.D.
Institute of Creation Research
Evidence for Creation
https://www.icr.org/article/845/313

The wonderful Tree of Life, discussed in the two "book ends" of the Bible, Genesis and Revelation, is one of the most fascinating (yet enigmatic) subjects in all the inspired word of God.

It is first mentioned in Genesis 2:9 - And out of the ground made the LORD God to grow every tree that is pleasant to the sight, and good for food; the tree of life also in the midst of the garden, and the tree of knowledge of good and evil.

It is pointless to speculate as to the exact nature of the Tree of Life, for God has not told us, and there is no tree like it in the present world. The same is true with reference to the Tree of Knowledge of Good and Evil.

God is well able to create any kind of tree He wishes, and we do well to leave it at that!

Because of the marvelous nature of the Tree of Life, however, the writer(s) of Proverbs used it (under divine inspiration of course) as a symbol of four wonderful truths.

First, the true wisdom "is a tree of life to them that lay hold upon her" (Proverbs 3:18). That true wisdom can be none other than Christ (I Corinthians 1:30, Colossians 2:3).

Second, "the fruit of the righteous is a tree of life" (Proverbs 11:30). Indeed, "the fruit of the Spirit is in all goodness and righteousness and truth" (Ephesians 5:9).

A life such as that will be like a tree of life to all who encounter it.

Third, "when the desire cometh, it is a tree of life" (Proverbs 13:12). That is, fulfilled hope, like true wisdom and righteousness is so vitalizing as to be a source of renewed vigorous life.

Fourth, "a wholesome tongue is a tree of life" (Proverbs 15:4). Therefore, "let your speech be always with grace, seasoned with salt, that ye may know how ye ought to answer every man" (Colossians 4:6).

We can eagerly, yet patiently and fruitfully, look forward to enjoying the delicious, nourishing fruit of the Tree of Life in the holy city someday.

In the meantime, we can pray that God will help us to be like little, life-giving trees ourselves through growing in true wisdom, living righteously, offering hope to the lost in our midst, and using our God-given abilities of communication graciously and meaningfully to all those we meet. (Morris, 1998)

The Tree of Life is also acquainted with hope:

> *Proverbs 13:12 - Hope deferred maketh the heart sick: but when the desire cometh, it is a tree of life.*

Hope is a powerful tool! If you have met someone who is without hope, they look depressed, sad and almost dead. The Tree of Life will give us hope!

Leaves for Healing of the Nations

I found an article that best describes this phenomenon as well:

Paul Taylor
The Healing Leaves

Many people, including myself have asked the question, "What do the leaves which are for the healing of the Nations mean in Revelation 22:2"?

I have studied the various scriptures which can be associated with this vision and arrived at the answers in this study. I do not claim to be 100 percent accurate as I am not a learned theologian, but with prayer and study I submit my findings.

In Rev. 22:2, John is shown a vision of a river with the tree of life planted on each side and bearing 12 manners of fruit, producing a different fruit each month, and the leaves of the tree are for the healing of the Nations.

You have a river ---You have trees---You have leaves, now, what do these symbols mean?

If we look in John 4:14 we see that Jesus is telling the woman at the well, that the water he gives is a well of water springing into eternal life. But whosoever drinketh of the water that I shall give him shall never thirst; but the water that I shall give him shall be in him a well of water springing up into everlasting life. So could the river in Johns vision be this well? Let's go to Zechariah 14:8

8 And it shall be in that day, that living waters shall go out from Jerusalem; half of them toward the former sea, and half of them toward the hinder sea: in summer and in winter shall it be. Jesus speaks to the woman at the well about a well of water offering eternal life; we then look at Zechariah 14:8 and we find another reference to living waters flowing from Jerusalem. By reading these two scriptures we can see they have a common bond in reference to the Living Waters, so there must be a connection. Remember what Revelation 22:2 had to say.

2. In the midst of the street of it, and on either side of the river, was there the tree of life, which bare twelve manners of fruits, and yielded her fruit every month: and the leaves of the tree were for the healing of the nations. Now we see three references to Waters, but, there is still another text that may give us a better understanding of the Living Waters. We find this text in Ezekiel 47:1-13.

We find Ezekiel is being shown a vision of the Temple, (in the New Jerusalem) where God will reside with his people forever.

The first thing Ezekiel sees are the water issuing from under the threshold of the Temple door, and near the altar on the south side. The guide in the vision then begins measuring 1000 cubit lengths and at each length the water becomes a little deeper; ankle deep, knee deep, loin deep and then it was impassable. Ezekiel was also shown these waters as a river with many trees lining each side which bare 12 kinds of fruit and bore a fruit each month, and leaves which would never fade.

I won't get into the four measurements which the guide was making, but will save it for a future lesson.

Are Zechariah, John, Ezekiel and Jesus speaking of the same thing? Zechariah said living waters would flow from Jerusalem, Ezekiel saw the living waters in his vision flowing from the Temple of God, John also saw nearly the identical vision in Revelation 22:2, Jesus told the woman at the well of the Living Waters which offered eternal life. So now we have 4 different references to the River of Life.

If we look at Ezekiel 47:8-9, we see the waters are flowing into the valleys and deserts, and wherever they flow all things are healed. The Greek word for healing is therapeia (there-ape-I'-ah) which means to cure. The waters then are as Jesus said, Living Waters which cure and grant eternal health and life.

Now, if the water is living water, healing everything it touches, then we see the trees along the banks which would, through their root system, tap into this life giving force, thereby passing it on to its fruit and leaves which would make the leaves a sort of medicine to the peoples and nations. Now we need to back up to the beginning and see if there is another clue to these visions and sayings.

We need to go back to Genesis 2:9-10 9 And out of the ground made the LORD God to grow every tree that is pleasant to the sight, and good for food; the TREE OF LIFE also in the midst of the garden, and the tree of knowledge of good and evil. 10 And a RIVER went out of Eden to water the garden; and from thence it was parted, and became into four heads.

Looking at these 2 verses we see (1)..Tree of Life , (2)..A river flowing from the Garden of Eden to water it.

Now if we look at the ending we see the beginning since the tree of life and the river of life are in both places, and water is flowing out from both places to give its life giving properties.

Let me see if I can put all this together and reach an explanation for the healing leaves of the tree of life.

Some commentators allude to the trees as being the saints and the fruit the word of God, which they are preaching to the multitudes prior to the second coming of Jesus; others are saying John is describing the raptured Christians living in Jerusalem during the 1000 year period following the rapture. I disagree with both of these theories, but will not debate them at this point for lack of space and time. When God placed Adam and Eve in the Garden of Eden to tend it and to worship him, he gave them the tree of life to eat from, which would have given them eternal life had they not rebelled and sinned against God.

73

There was a river flowing out of Eden, which watered and gave life to all of God's creation. The climate was perfect, there was no death, violence, dangerous carnivorous animals, (animals were vegetarian, see (Genesis 1:30) sickness, or diseases in this world which God had created. The tree of Life and the river flowing from Eden were to sustain all of God's creation for eternity, but humankind being humankind believed the grass was greener on the other side.

Reflecting on Eden, couldn't we conclude that the river flowing from Eden, and the River flowing from the Temple in Ezekiel 47:1, the river in Revelation 22:2 with the trees lining the river which runs through the city, and the tree of Life in the Garden of Eden in Genesis 2:9, be one and the same, giving life sustaining substance to God's people in the beginning and the end. Now let's take a look at the leaf of these trees which Ezekiel, and John describes as healing the Nations.

What is a leaf and what is its purpose?

A leaf is a sort of reservoir and conduit for life giving properties to the tree and its fruits.

A leaf with its surface area captures the sunlight, water, and carbon dioxide and through photosynthesis converts these into oxygen and sugar to feed the tree. This energy and nutrients are fed to the tree, which in turn passes these nutrients to the fruit and on to the one which consumes the fruits. Leaves begin to fade and drop off the trees in autumn due to the lack of sunlight as the days become shorter. In the New Jerusalem there will be no need for sunlight as Jesus's Glory will give the light as shown in Revelation 21:23, therefore the leaves will never FADE or drop as the light from the Lamb will never dim. 23 And the city had no need of the sun, neither of the moon, to shine in it: for the glory of God did lighten it, and the Lamb is the light thereof.

Let's review some of the texts and see if we can arrive at a possible answer.

> *John 4:14 - the water that I shall give him he shall never thirst.*
>
> *Zechariah 14:8 that living waters shall go out from Jerusalem,*
>
> *Revelation 22:1-2*
>
> *1 And he shewed me a pure river of water of life, clear as crystal, proceeding out of the throne of God and of the Lamb.*
>
> *2 In the midst of the street of it, and on either side of the river, was there the tree of life, which bare twelve manner of fruits, and yielded her fruit every month: and the leaves of the tree were for the healing of the nations..*
>
> *Ezekiel 47:12 And by the river upon the bank thereof, on this side and on that side, shall grow all trees for meat, whose leaf shall not fade,. and the fruit thereof shall be for meat, and the LEAF thereof for MEDICINE*
>
> *Revelation 21:23 And the city had no need of the sun, neither of the moon, to shine in it: for the glory of God did lighten it, and the Lamb is the light thereof*

We know that water is the essence of life and we must consume a certain amount daily in order to survive, so we can surmise that the river and the water spoken of in these verses are the same and possess a divinely created miraculous healing and sustaining ability of which we can't imagine.

I believe the river of water in the New Jerusalem, as well as the river which ran out from Eden has the same properties. If they have the same life sustaining properties, then it stands to reason that the trees lining the river will get their sustenance from this water as well as from the leaves which will absorb the Light of Glory from the Lamb as indicated in Revelation 21:23.

This being the case then, is it not possible that the leaves, by absorbing the Light of the Lamb, and the roots absorbing the life sustaining force of the river, channeling it to the fruit of the trees, which in turn transfers all of this to the nations consuming the fruit, be the medicine for healing the Nations as described in Revelation 22:2? I base this on the fact that Jesus did eat after his resurrection; also the Angels who visited Abraham ate solid food.

In the Old Testament, angels ate when Abraham entertained them (Genesis 18:8). Jesus ate after He rose from the dead (Luke 24:41-43).

We will also eat as indicated in Isaiah 65:21. 21 And they shall build houses, and inhabit them; and they shall plant vineyards, and eat the fruit of them.

We know from scientific fact, and studies that a balanced and healthy diet has a direct relationship to the disposition of the mentality of the human brain. Those that stay on a junk food or unhealthy diet tend to become, and stay angry, disgruntled, lower intelligence and creating conflict when conflict is not necessary. On the other hand those on a well-balanced healthy diet tend to be level headed, of higher intellectual ability, and morally stronger, avoiding and or settling disputes in a rational and just way. Then the miraculous eternal life giving nutrients from the Tree of Life would be a perfectly balanced diet for Gods people, as God makes all things perfect.

In conclusion it would appear that the leaves through their conversion of Gods light, and the water from the river of life, heals the nations by its medicinal properties being passed onto the fruit of the trees. I am not saying I'm correct in my assessment of this vision which John saw of the tree of life and the healing of the Nation's properties of the leaves, but, I request others to diligently study this and possibly enhance on this study, or show me to be totally wrong.

I am merely seeking the truth without any sugarcoating or left field analysis not being Biblically based. (Taylor, 2012)

Rev.11/19/12 Copyright 2012

All Rights Reserved Paul L. Taylor

Paul Taylor Granted Permissions for This Article Submission

Paul Taylor a Christian writer attempting to get the truth out to the masses before it is too late

Article Source: http://www.faithwriters.com

Dr. Dianna Senkyrik from Eagleheart Ministries in Bay City Texas says that when she is about to pray for someone in healing that God will show her the Tree of Life in the spirit. She says it has gold leaves and she just reaches up in the spirit and grabs one of those leaves and applies it to people for their healing. Isn't that amazing?

This is the main scripture of all about the Tree of Life:

> **Revelation 2:7 - He that hath an ear, let him hear what the Spirit saith unto the churches; To him that overcometh will I give to eat of the tree of life, which is in the midst of the paradise of God.**

See more in the *Clarion Call to Unity* book.

7

HUMANS ARE TREES?

When God created man, He created them from the dust of the
Earth, within the garden. He then breathed into man. We contain
the breath of God. He designed us to be a replica of His image.

This is a visual of how we are symbolically like trees in God's
Great Garden:

How are we a Tree?

When God created man, he created them and then placed them
in the Garden of Eden. He created them out of the dust of the earth
and breathed LIFE into them out of his breath. God designed the
man to possess a seed, just like plants. At mating time, the male
will insert his seed into a woman.   At conception and
impregnation, the seed fertilizes the woman's egg, which then
develops into a fetus inside of her womb.

Thus, LIFE begins at the moment of conception. This seed is
then embedded within a sack of water inside a living tree. The
growing plant inside the big tree feeds off of the adult tree and
matures to full expectancy.

While it is in the womb, it is attached to the Tree of Life. It
receives its nourishment off of its creator. It is attached to the vine
inside the mother and feeds off the good tree.

It is protected within the waters and wrapped in dirt. It is
underneath the ground and struggling as it's growing to plunge
through the Earthly dirt and be revealed into the atmosphere.

The environment of the mother tree will affect the little plant inside her. As it travels through the matrix and is exposed to the earthly realm, it is then subject to the environment and surroundings.

As the young plant comes through the birth canal, it is birthed into the new atmosphere of the garden and is released into the atmosphere outside of the womb; the tree is now birthed into the garden as a dead, dry tree. The only fruit that tree can bear is from it's carnal nature. It's fruit it is like dried up raisins.

When that plant enters the Earth-realm, it is still attached to the womb of the mother tree, or shall we say attached to the vine. Until the cord is severed, the child feeds off its mother. When the child is seperated from its mother tree, it must survive in this unfamiliar atmosphere.

This young baby plant at that point survives off of the mother's breasts until it can be fed food from the Earth. At this point, the tree is learning behaviors and the patterns that the mother tree and environment are training it to believe. Unless the parent trees or the environment guides that tree to God, it may not find its way to the creator unless someone else is praying for that tree.

Isaiah 11:1-5

1 And there shall come forth a rod out of the stem of Jesse, and a Branch shall grow out of his roots:

2 And the spirit of the Lord shall rest upon him, the spirit of wisdom and understanding, the spirit of counsel and might, the spirit of knowledge and of the fear of the Lord;

3 And shall make him of quick understanding in the fear of the Lord: and he shall not judge after the sight of his eyes, neither reprove after the hearing of his ears:

4 But with righteousness shall he judge the poor, and reprove with equity for the meek of the earth: and he shall smite the earth: with the rod of his mouth, and with the breath of his lips shall he slay the wicked.

5 And righteousness shall be the girdle of his loins, and faithfulness the girdle of his reins.

Most fruit trees cannot reproduce on their own. They must have other trees around them to pollinate. They need other trees around them to reproduce the fruit or otherwise it would just grow pretty flowers.

Also, I learned in college that the prettier the flower, the more sexual it is. It is that pretty to attract the bees so that it can be pollinated. It's amazing how God created nature.

Until the tree connects with its creator, it may have all types of baggage. It may be wrecked with diseases, viruses, bumps, knots, bitter roots, etc. When that tree realizes the need for its creator, it submits its tree back to Him and repents for the sin.

Salvation – A Supernatural Experience

Once a tree repents and humbles to the creator and accepts the sacrifice of Jesus for its sins, then the roots supernaturally connect to Heaven. He is the vine, and we are the branches:

When God created the Earth He separated the waters to make Earth and Heaven. In the beginning, the waters were all one.

81

God is the one who made the divide and separated them.

Think about it, when it rains on Earth its water coming from the heavens. We are in between these two water sources. So, when our tree connects with the creator in the heavenly realm, our roots supernaturally connect to the rivers of living water.

When our roots connect to the living rivers, we supernaturally connect to the spiritual vine and begin to bear good living fruit. Our tree comes alive, and we are born into a new realm and reality.

We step out of the natural realm of just LIFE in the dead dry world, entering into a living water world in the spiritual supernatural realm. Think about how the Bible says to let the rivers flow through us to the world.

Sometimes you can look into someone's eyes and see that they are hollow or empty. Other times you can look into someone's eyes and see the rivers. You can feel the peace and the anointing upon them.

John 15:1-11

1 I am the true vine, and my Father is the husbandman.

2 Every branch in me that beareth not fruit he taketh away: and every branch that beareth fruit, he purgeth it, that it may bring forth more fruit.

3 Now ye are clean through the word which I have spoken unto you.

4 Abide in me, and I in you. As the branch cannot bear fruit of itself, except it abide in the vine; no more can ye, except ye abide in me.

5 I am the vine, ye are the branches: He that abideth in me, and I in him, the same bringeth forth much fruit: for without me ye can do nothing.

6 If a man abide not in me, he is cast forth as a branch, and is withered; and men gather them, and cast them into the fire, and they are burned.

7 If ye abide in me, and my words abide in you, ye shall ask what ye will, and it shall be done unto you.

8 Herein is my Father glorified, that ye bear much fruit; so shall ye be my disciples.

9 As the Father hath loved me, so have I loved you: continue ye in my love.

10 If ye keep my commandments, ye shall abide in my love; even as I have kept my Father's commandments, and abide in his love.

11 These things have I spoken unto you, that my joy might remain in you, and that your joy might be full.

John 7:37-38

37 In the last day, that great day of the feast, Jesus stood and cried, saying, If any man thirst, let him come unto me, and drink.

38 He that believeth on me, as the scripture hath said, out of his belly shall flow rivers of living water.

Interesting Facts about Humans Compared to Trees:

- We are born from a seed = the seed goes back to the dirt and dies and then brings resurrection life. Must die to bring life!
- Cultivated in the womb in water
    - Represents Rivers of living water...the seed is protected in those waters! Warm, secure, grows and is refreshed.
    - Connected to the mother tree through the umbilical cord! Feeding off that tree!

Born into a sin world and sin nature
    - Thus makes us a withered tree
    - Birthing pains are painful birthing the tree into the Earth in God's Great Garden
    - When delivered, everything that carried that tree gets discarded out of womb, then tree is restored
    - We have no nourishment except from worldly system/law and adult tree caretaker
    - We are feeding off of the Tree of Knowledge of Good and Evil because Satan is the god of this world and the world is ran by him. We are born into deceit.

When we are saved, our roots supernaturally connect to Rivers of Living Water/Jesus. When God separated the waters, when we get saved, our roots connect to the heavenly flow.
    - Then our tree flourishes
    - Our roots dig down into the rivers

- Nourishes our tree through the word and His presence
- It's like being connected through the umbilical cord to the original creator! He is now our nourisher! He is the vine and we are the branches!
- God wants to talk to us like He did Adam and Eve in the Garden. We are supernaturally back in the Garden!
- His son Jesus shines on us and we need to be in His presence for growth
- The son is nourishment – photosynthesis supernaturally

God created Adam in a garden, the Garden of Eden
- He created Eve from the side of Adam
- We were created from dirt...like a plant!
- We were a flourishing tree from creation because Adam walked with God
- When they ate of the wrong tree (Knowledge of Good and Evil), then their tree dried up and we became of the Law.

As parents we have knowledge of bad things on Earth and we don't want our kids knowing it either so we protect them from that knowledge.

- When Jesus came, he reconnected us to the Vine and the Rivers of Living Water!
- Now we have all access as we did in the Garden of Eden!
- God looks at us like a garden like Song of Solomon talks about...that's like God's love for us!
- He had to die on a tree to match his Bride!
- God gave Jesus the Bride! The trees in the garden!
- The roots flop around in the rivers receiving nourishment,

- o This keeps our heart soft and clean before God
- It also allows us to RELEASE to others that river of love, the Holy Ghost, etc.
- Offense is number one tool of enemy to clog your roots.
- If you don't protect the eye-gate, ear-gate & mouth-gate, it will clog our roots as well.
- Roots
  - o Offense, sin, etc., will allow spirits to come in and clog our roots.
  - o Dries up the well so we can't receive
  - o Then spirit goes back up vein into the heart and slows down the heart and makes it hard and separated from God.
  - o Roots of bitterness, etc., rotten roots will prevent them from sloshing around in freedom in the waters.

Heart

- o Out of the heart the mouth speaks
- o Heart is wicked...can't trust it
- o Demons reside in heart and tries to guide it
- o Holy Spirit can search a man's heart
- o God judges the heart because only He can see in it. The tree may be hard, and pretty. But heart is exposed to God.

Just as there are 18 different types of fruits, there are many different types of humans. We are many colors, shapes, sizes, etc. This reveals in a small part how big and vast our God is. God cannot be contained within a box or be limited to only one certain color! He is all of us. We are a composite of God, who made us.

Our Trees Are Unique

One time I preached in a men's prison and I asked each nationality to represent their race and come up front. They were happy to do so. I was preaching about trees and how they are all unique in God's eyes. I explained that trees do not have a choice where planted or the environment they're planted in, but they are still planted on this Earth for a reason. Well, when it came time to call them up front, they proudly lined up from one side of the chapel to the other.

They faced the other prisoners as I walked to the back of the room and I stood in between the other prisoners who were sitting down. I said, "OK, look closely at the men. Pay attention to the different colors of their skins. Look at the shape of their faces. Look at how tall or short they are. Look at the leaves at the top of their tree. (They laughed). I want you all to notice the different types of trees that God created! Now you see God! He's all those colors and shapes! Only we try to put Him in a box and say He looks a certain way. We are ALL created in His image."

Then I instructed the crowd to stand when their respective nationality was called out. I held the microphone to the first man and said, "What nation do you represent?" He said, "Cherokee Indians." Then all the Cherokee's would stand up and shout. Each nationality proudly responded.

During the altar call, they lined up from the front to the back of the church for me to pray with them. The first man said, "My tree has been bad." I laughed and said, "OK, well let's make that right with God." I then prayed the sinner's prayer with him. The next prisoner humbly said, "My tree has demons." So, I pulled him aside and cast the demons out of him. As each one approached me, they all recognized that their trees were unique and needed healing so that they can bear much fruit for God.

A Hollow Tree/Evil Tree

Have you ever seen a hollow tree? Ever looked into someone's eyes and no one is at home? I know I have many times. Eyes are the window to the soul.

Most of the time when demons are active in a tree, you can see them through the eyes, or eye-gate. You can see evil through pupils.

When one's eye pupils are huge, it usually reflects demonic activity. Just watch someone when they get angry about something or they talk about something that happened and you can tell they have not forgiven those people, their pupils get real big. This knowledge is based on my years of experience with casting demons out. The tree can be full of demons, or it can be filled with the God the Holy Spirit. When we surrender our tree to God and allow Him to fill us with His presence and Holy Spirit, then He fills our tree with the fullness of His glory.

However, I do want to say that although we get saved, it does not mean that we are free of all demons. Some demons will hide and we need to go through deliverance to be free from them. For instance, it's like peeling an onion back. We continually get healed by God one layer at a time. The Bible says we are to renew our mind and wash it with the water of the word. It cleans our hearts and souls out. It's like a supernatural car wash. It supernaturally searches the innermost parts and reveals things that we need healed of. Once we confess those things to God He will bring healing. This subject is for another book. However, I just wanted to point out that our hearts are forever being conditioned and healed by God. We may not realize we have issues but God will bring those to the surface so that we can be healed and He can operate through us more efficiently. Like the car wash, He continually washes underneath the hood, wheels, trunk, etc.

Matthew 6:22 - The light of the body is the eye: if therefore thine eye be single, thy whole body shall be full of light.

Am I a Good or Bad Tree?

The Bible refers to us as trees many times. It talks about us bearing fruit for God and if we do not, and then God will be forced to throw our tree in the fire because we were of no use in His Great Garden.

Matthew 7:17-20

17 Even so every good tree bringeth forth good fruit; but a corrupt tree bringeth forth evil fruit.

18 A good tree cannot bring forth evil fruit, neither can a corrupt tree bring forth good fruit.

19 Every tree that bringeth not forth good fruit is hewn down, and cast into the fire.

20 Wherefore by their fruits ye shall know them.

Two Trees Standing Before the Throne on Judgment Day

BAD TREE

"God, I wanted my tree to myself because I wanted to be selfish and do what I wanted to with my tree. It's my LIFE, and I didn't want to pay the price you require to be in the GREAT GARDEN. I wanted to create my garden and do my own thing. I knew I only live once on this earth, and I wanted to do my LIFE the way I wanted to."

Then God responds, "I created this garden for you to enjoy. You did not enjoy the birds, the trees, the sky, or anything that I created for you. You were too busy serving the god of the world, and you made the choice to reject my son, so I have no choice but to throw your tree in the fire. You were of no use to Me in the Great Garden. You didn't bear any fruit for Me or reproduce after my kind. You reproduced after Satan's carnal world and led many people on the wrong path. You ate of the Tree of Knowledge of Good and Evil, thus I must kick you out of My garden. Get away from Me for I never knew you."

Proverbs 11:30 - The fruit of the righteous is a tree of life; and he that winneth souls is wise.

GOOD TREE -

Just like the other tree, this tree will stand before God and plead its case, "I surrendered my tree to you, and I reproduced fruit after your kind and produced much fruit for you God. There were many times I stood under judgment from you on Earth as you corrected, rebuked, chastised and instructed me. I kept my heart clean from offense, sin, and the god of the world. I keep my communication lines and my roots open to the Heavens to keep my tree pure."

Then God looks at this tree and says, "Because you burned with My Holy fire on Earth and reproduced souls after My kind and produced much fruit and gave Me glory with your tree, then you are free to enter My kingdom to rule and reign with me. You allowed me to continually purge and cleanse your tree, thus your tree was able to grow tall and bear so much fruit for my Kingdom. Well done thy good and faithful servant."

Matthew 12:33 - Either make the tree good, and his fruit good; or else make the tree corrupt, and his fruit corrupt: for the tree is known by his fruit.

How Do You Take Care of Your Tree?

Your tree receives its nourishment through the Word of God. It is through the washing of the word as the Bible says. The Word is our food and cleanser. Check this out:

Ephesians 5:26 – That he might sanctify and cleanse it with the washing of water by the word

Jeremiah 15:16 - Thy words were found, and I did eat them; and thy word was unto me the joy and rejoicing of mine heart: for I am called by thy name, O LORD God of hosts.

Hebrews 4:12 –- For the word of God is quick, and powerful, and sharper than any two-edged sword, piercing even to the dividing asunder of soul and spirit, and of the joints and marrow, and is a discerner of the thoughts and intents of the heart.

Deuteronomy 8:3 –- And he humbled thee, and suffered thee to hunger, and fed thee with manna, which thou knewest not, neither did thy fathers know; that he might make thee know that man doth not live by bread only, but by every word that proceedeth out of the mouth of the Lord doth man live.

We nourish our tree through reading the Bible, prayer, praise, and living in and sharing God's love.

Colossians 2:7 –- Rooted and built up in him, and stablished in the faith, as ye have been taught, abounding therein with thanksgiving.

We keep our tree in the presence of the sun for nourishment. Of course, I mean SON as in the Son of the Living God – Jesus! When we spend time with our creator, He refreshes our tree and he shines His glory upon us. The sun provides heat, energy, and nourishment to plants. Without the sun, most plants will die.

We keep our roots cleaned out and refreshed for the rivers of living water.

When a person (tree) gets saved, the roots open up to the heavenly realm and begin receiving nourishment from the river of living waters flowing out from under the throne of God. They flow easily and freely like open pipes when the human walks in humility and forgiveness. When they keep their heart clean, the rivers flow.

Dream About Sin in a Tree

I saw a tree in a forest. It was a big, pretty ole tree'. It had lots of fruit on it and just looked like a happy, proud fruit tree. I saw the sun shining on its top, and the tree loved its warmth and love. The tree was a satisfied 'ole tree growing in the glory.

Well, one day I saw a big arrow flying towards it and on the outside of the arrow it said, "Offense." The tree reached out a branch and pushed that arrow away. The tree said, "I forgive!"

Then I saw another yet bigger and wider arrow coming towards the tree. It said, "BIG OFFENSE." Well, the tree looked at it and knew this arrow hurt so deep that he didn't want to stop that arrow.

This offense cut deep into the heart of the tree. He allowed that arrow to penetrate his tree. The arrow pierced his trunk and made a big gaping wound in the tree. The tip of the arrow went all the way to the heart of the tree.

When the arrow hit the heart I saw a black thing (looked like a spirit) come out of the tip of the arrow and go down the veins to the roots. When it got to the roots that were flowing easy and soft in the river, it clogged the roots and made it hard.

Then I saw the rivers of life-giving waters trying to enter the roots of the tree but it couldn't because this spirit had blocked it. Then the spirit climbed back up to the heart and embedded in the heart. When it did, I saw the heart slow down its beating.

In the dream, I saw the heart before the spirit entered. It was pink, fleshy and soft. It beat perfectly before the Lord.
But when the spirit entered the heart it slowed it down like it was drying it up

(Out of the heart the mouth speaks!)

Then I saw arrow after arrow attacking the tree! Because it had opened up the first wound, it opened the door to the other arrows. I knew those arrows were many more things: I knew the arrows meant more offense, seeing things the tree should not be looking at, hearing things it should not be hearing, etc. In other words, it opened up all the other gates to the heart such as the eye gate, ear gate, and mouth gate.

When I saw all the arrows hitting the tree, I saw the spirits coming out of the bottom tip of the arrows and going down to the roots and clogging them up. I saw the tree drying up and the roots hitting the heart and it shriveling up like a hard ball. The heart stopped beating, became hard as stone, the rivers quit flowing, the fruits dried up on the tree, the leaves started falling off, and the tree became hard and stiff.

The once beautiful tree, which had long stood in God's beautiful sunshine, purposefully stepped out from under the rays of God's Sonshine. After it stepped into the darkness of the forest, it eventually looked like a rotten tree, in eternal death.

This tree reminds me of humans and their choices. We make a choice to get saved and give God our LIFE. We also make choices to continue in our sin and to stay out from under the glory of God.

This is how the tree was to the sunshine above it. The once glory it loved to stand under became bitterness to the tree, and it chose to abandon the light.

As you can visualize, the first open gaping wound opened up the door for the other arrows.

The Lord gave me this dream right before I preached in a women's prison. I was able to tell these women that God brought me there to help them to clean their pipes and heal their roots. We must all forgive.

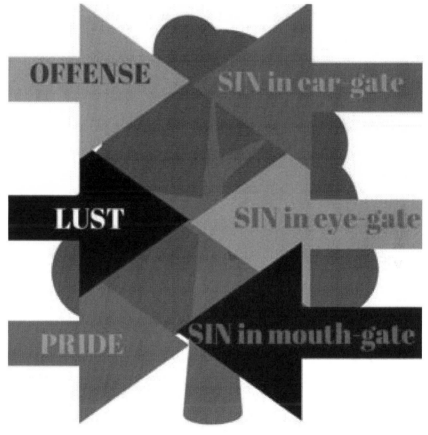

Most trees do not have the choice of where they are planted. Some are on rocky soil, flooded soil, dry soil, or they may have birds that poop on them all the time.

They may have bees that build nests in them, etc. They did not have the choice if they're a beautiful fruit tree or an ugly tree that no one wants to see.

We Are All Mighty Oaks

One day I was leaving a person's home and noticed two trees in the front yard. They both looked like big oak trees. One was beautiful, fluffy, with nice thick bark, a strong trunk and limbs, healthy green leaves, etc. It looks like a picture-perfect tree. But the other tree next to it in the same yard was skinny, missing half its bark, scraggly looking trunk and half missing limbs. It looked very sick, anemic as if it had viruses and was just an ugly tree.

So, I looked at the big fluffy, pretty one and said, "Wow! You are such an awesome, beautiful tree! I bet you get compliments all the time!" Then I looked at the other tree and said, "Awe…you poor tree. I bet no one looks at you because of this other beautiful massive tree. I'm sorry." After I left that night, God gave me a dream. I preached that sermon at the nursing home that week called, **"We are ALL Mighty Oaks to God!"**

How Tree Comes to LIFE and
Connect to the Rivers of Living Water

Until this tree discovers God as their Ultimate Gardener and attaches itself back to the vine…it remains wounded, headed for death.

But when it connects to the true vine…then…the roots supernaturally go down into the rivers of living water that comes from Jesus and Heaven. Our roots then begin to enter another dimension of power, laws, rules, and kingdom! This realm is the Kingdom of God.

Those roots are firmly placed into the REAL LIFE SOURCE. Currently we are on this alien planet and only here for a short time.

Now those waters fill our tree from the bottom up...which is why we say, I'm overflowing- Fill me up Lord! God wants those rivers to come out of us. It's the anointing, the glory - COME OUT!

OK...now our roots are firmly attached to the Heavenly Jesus vine. We are the branches, and Jesus is the vine. Now that we have the LIFE giving flow...we can bear much fruit if we trust God with our lives so that we can bear that fruit!

The Lord gave me a dream on November 11, 2013:
Dream - Finish the Race

In this life we do struggle as we make decisions in our lives. But it's not about how you begin the race it's how you finish the race.

It is about how you finish the race. My dad had a very sad life he was an alcoholic and a very sad man but the last 10 years of his life, he changed his life and dedicated to the Lord. He finished the race and beheld his face.

It's not about how you began because a lot of us have sin and have sad stories so today is the beginning of the rest of your life. How will you finish the race? How will you finish the race? We never know the time or hour when we show cross over to the other side. Choose this day to you will serve.

When you finish the race, you shall behold his face. His face lights the heavens. His face is glorious. Your eyes shall behold him. He will take you by the hand and take you to your mansion. He has created a beautiful home for you. Your home will be everything you dreamed of as a child. It will be beyond your wildest dreams. The colors are light just for a glorious.

It's not how you began the race; it is how you finished the race. The Lord desires to use you in a marvelous way. He just has to line you up.

As you have prayed for God's line of your children and your children's destinies, and lining of your destiny, I Must pluck it all out so that you may be a tall tree standing firm in me. I will heal you says the Lord of all your distresses.

Trust in me my child for greater is he that is in you then he that is in the world. How much I love you my daughter. How I desire to bless you immensely. You shall not be ashamed.

Bear Much Fruit for God with Our Tree
Fruit that will Remain

Just as we are going back to the Garden and connecting our tree to the Tree of Life, we will bear much fruit for Him in the Kingdom of God.

The Lord gave me this dream on November 22, 2014:

Dream about Tree of Life

I was in my new house and I was standing on my back deck looking into the back yard. There was a beautiful tree right in the middle that had all different types of fruit growing from it. I mean it had bananas, Apples, oranges and different fruits.

I ran out the back porch to eat one fruit. As I ate it, the tree automatically grew another one. So, I kept eating and it kept growing.

I saw like the house full of people and they were looking at this tree in amazement. They couldn't believe all the fruit that grew on that tree. They yelled, "We want a banana. We want an apple." The more I gave away, it gave me more and very easily. Then the tree kept growing taller and thicker and it grew up through the clouds.

When I needed a fruit, I put my hands around my mouth and yelled to top of my lungs and tell it what I needed and with ease it would bend down and give it to me! It was no effort pulling that fruit off the tree.

It was very apparent to the guests how blessed I am with all this fruit! As much as it would release, I would GIVE IT away. I kept hearing, FRUIT THAT WILL REMAIN. FRUIT THAT WILL REMAIN."

Then I woke up and the Lord gave me these scriptures. (He often does with my dreams/visions).

> *John 15:1-11*
>
> *1 I am the true vine, and my Father is the husbandman.*
>
> *2 Every branch in me that beareth not fruit he taketh away: and every branch that beareth fruit, he purgeth it, that it may bring forth more fruit.*
>
> *3 Now ye are clean through the word which I have spoken unto you.*
>
> *4 Abide in me, and I in you. As the branch cannot bear fruit of itself, except it abide in the vine; no more can ye, except ye abide in me.*
>
> *5 I am the vine, ye are the branches: He that abideth in me, and I in him, the same bringeth forth much fruit: for without me ye can do nothing.*

6 If a man abide not in me, he is cast forth as a branch, and is withered; and men gather them, and cast them into the fire, and they are burned.

7 If ye abide in me, and my words abide in you, ye shall ask what ye will, and it shall be done unto you.

8 Herein is my Father glorified, that ye bear much fruit; so shall ye be my disciples.

9 As the Father hath loved me, so have I loved you: continue ye in my love.

10 If ye keep my commandments, ye shall abide in my love; even as I have kept my Father's commandments, and abide in his love.

11 These things have I spoken unto you, that my joy might remain in you, and that your joy might be full.

John 15:16 - You did not choose Me but I chose you, and appointed you that you would go and bear fruit, and that your fruit would remain, so that whatever you ask of the Father in My name He may give to you.

Notes about dream

The fruit looked so big colorful and juicy. The more I gave away, the tree kept growing taller. When I needed a fruit, it would bend down so I could pick it off with such ease! There were many people going in and out of that house and I was blessing them with this fruit. It was obvious and apparent to them how blessed I was.

8

TYPES OF SEEDS
IN THE GARDEN

The Bible talks about many different types of seeds. He speaks of seeds because it is the beginning of life.

> *Genesis 8:22 - While the earth remaineth, seedtime and harvest, and cold and heat, and summer and winter, and day and night shall not cease.*

Everything needs to be planted in order to grow. The Lord wants us to use our resources to bring things about in this earthly realm. We are conduits for His will, thus He needs us to act and to make things happen. All He requires is that we release the seeds. He is responsible for watering and cultivating the seeds for growth. This is why He should be the only one receiving glory. We are only part of a body or part of a team.

The following is a blog I wrote on July 26, 2014

You are the Conduit

You are the avenue in which God is using to bring victory to another human on this planet. I know this sounds strange, but our battle is not with flesh and blood; but with the principalities and the powers of the air. We battle in the spirit realm.

We fight against the wickedness that is ruling on the Earth today.

Remember, we are on this Earth but operate in the Kingdom of Heaven.

This means that we have tools, keys that we can use to change the atmosphere! How do we change the atmosphere? By our mouths! By our words! We declare things to shift in the atmosphere. It is so important to watch our words....the Bible says out of our mouths speak life and death, curses and blessings. We can literally bring sickness on ourselves by our own mouths and confessions. Protect this instrument

So, this is why praying in tongues is such a key and a weapon for Christians. We pray in that beautiful heavenly language that only God understands. It's the Holy Spirit within us speaking in the atmosphere His will on Earth. It is more important for us to pray in tongues than it is in English. This ensures that when we pray in English that it does not come from the soul-realm, but the spirit-realm. It packs more power when spirit-led.

People say they don't know how to pray...then they need to get filled with the Holy Ghost. He will teach them how to pray. He is our perfect teacher and guide. When you are filled with the Holy Ghost and you don't know what to pray in English...then pray in tongues and let the Holy Ghost lead you.

Back to salvation prayers...here is great wisdom I learned last year in my fiery trial:

When God chooses you to be the conduit and to pray for someone's salvation, you are immediately stepping into warfare. The devil does not want Jane saved. What God revealed to me that happens when we pray for salvation, healing, deliverance, etc., on someone is this:

June: God, I'm believing you to change Jane! Heal her heart Lord! Save her, cause her to be in your most perfect will. I call out her destiny within her to come to full fruition through you Lord!

I call forth the greatness on the inside of her. I speak salvation to her, healing, and the fullness of your presence. Lord, I pray you give her an encounter with you that she can never deny who you are. I pray you send laborers across her path to help her to reach her true destiny on that narrow path Lord. I call the angels from Heaven to move on her behalf and to dispel the darkness from her life.

I command all spiritual warfare, spells, incantations, negative words, or anything not of God to be removed from her life. I plead the blood of Jesus over her and thank you right now for her salvation Lord! I command every mountain hindering her life to be removed!

OK…so now I've brought my petition before God in the spirit. I've boldly entered the throne room on her behalf. I have asked the creator of the universe to pinpoint this human and move on her behalf! So, I have favor with God because his word says that the prayers of the righteous availeth much.

God says, "OK angels deliver this prayer to Earth." Angels are heading down to Earth.

Devil sees it coming. He knows what is going on. (Especially if I've prayed it in English and not my tongues).

He tells his demons, "Go to Jane and cause her to bring offense to June that only Jane can do!"

So Jane offends me. My flesh gets so riled up because she hit me right where it hurts!

I have a choice to make at that moment. There are two roads that can be taken here:

A. Take the offense and speak against what I have been believing God for because my pride has been hurt and HOW DARE THEM! LOL. Basically, when we hold an offense to someone we are holding God back from moving because we were the conduit HE was using to begin with. It also harms that person too. We want them to be FREE more than we want to be offended. It's not about us...it's about SOULS!

B. We can choose to immediately forgive that person and give them to God. This is the best option because we should fear for that person that harms us. So, we must pray mercy and grace upon that person. We are special to God and He will hold someone greatly accountable that hurts us. Also, we want them to be free!!!

I shared that blog because it reflects how our prayers are seeds planted for another person's destiny. If we take offense and turn our back on believing God for someone else, the devil wins. We must be wise to Satan's tactics.

Faith Seed

Most of the time we make it happen by faith. A lot of things are brought into the natural realm when we activate our faith. In order to see what we believe God for we must release a faith seed (faith as a grain of mustard seed). The Bible talks about this faith seed:

> *Matthew 17:20 - And Jesus said unto them, Because of your unbelief: for verily I say unto you, If ye have faith as a grain of mustard seed, ye shall say unto this mountain, Remove hence to yonder place; and it shall remove; and nothing shall be impossible unto you.*

It makes you wonder why God calls faith a seed. How can faith move a mountain with just a seed? It is because He needs us to take a step (seed) of faith. Think about all the miracles in the Bible.

They start out by the person doing something to receive. Moses had to cast his rod into the waters in order to cross to the other side. Peter had to walk on the water to get to Jesus. The blind man had to rub mud in his eyes. The lame man had to jump in the pool at Bethesda, etc. It is all based upon them stepping when they do not see the miracle. When God sees them doing what they can then He does the rest.

Financial Seeds

I know there are many people that do not believe in prosperity for Christians. Some believe that Christians are taking a vow of poverty because Jesus was not rich. However, that mentality negates the fact of how God blessed His people with wealth. Look at Solomon, Abraham, etc. We are Abraham's Seed, thus we are the heirs to his promise. God is a good daddy. He says in His word that His seed shall not be begging bread. We are blessed coming in and blessed coming out. Even Jesus talked about how we are heirs to the promise.

Galatians 3:5-7, 14, 16-19, 26-29

5 He therefore that ministereth to you the Spirit, and worketh miracles among you, doeth he it by the works of the law, or by the hearing of faith?

6 Even as Abraham believed God, and it was accounted to him for righteousness.

7 Know ye therefore that they which are of faith, the same are the children of Abraham.

16 Now to Abraham and his seed were the promises made. He saith not, And to seeds, as of many; but as of one, And to thy seed, which is Christ.

17 And this I say, that the covenant, that was confirmed before of God in Christ, the law, which was four hundred and thirty years after, cannot disannul, that it should make the promise of none effect.

18 For if the inheritance be of the law, it is no more of promise: but God gave it to Abraham by promise.

19 Wherefore then serveth the law? It was added because of transgressions, till the seed should come to whom the promise was made; and it was ordained by angels in the hand of a mediator.

26 For ye are all the children of God by faith in Christ Jesus.

27 For as many of you as have been baptized into Christ have put on Christ.

28 There is neither Jew nor Greek, there is neither bond nor free, there is neither male nor female: for ye are all one in Christ Jesus.

29 And if ye be Christ's, then are ye Abraham's seed, and heirs according to the promise.

We are heirs to the promise and Abraham had many blessings from God:

> *Genesis 12:7 - "And the Lord appeared unto Abram, and said, Unto thy seed will I give this land: and there builded he an altar unto the Lord, who appeared unto him."*

Abraham's blessings are many and won't list in this book, but we are considered his seed and have access to those blessings!

Another seed is in tithing. God wants our ten percent back to Him for blessing us. Just remember that money is not evil, it's the love of money that is evil.

> *1 Timothy 6:10 - For the love of money is the root of all evil: which while some coveted after, they have erred from the faith, and pierced themselves through with many sorrows.*

Tithing is a principal by God which provides many protections as well. You can never out-give God

My mother says to this day (she is 75) that God takes care of her in old age because she tithed all those years. The sowing and reaping concept applies in giving financially as well. In any need you have, sow it to receive from it. If you need more love, sow love. If you need more money, sow money. So, money is a seed; a financial seed.

Family Trees and Seeds

Please notice the picture on the next page. It is a family tree of a family in Necaise, Mississippi. Take notice of the one branch that was short stub because the life was cut short. This picture accurately displays how family trees work.

The Bible uses several descriptions for the family tree. The father carries a seed, then the mother births the seed, and together their seed is called offspring.

The Bible refers to parts of plants with humans. For instance, He said, "The stem of Jesse" referring to David. The seed of Abraham, seeds, flowers, etc. In referring to a family tree, God talks about the seed needing to continue to grow and multiply.

He also speaks about seed dying. See this:

Mark 12:19-22

19 Master, Moses wrote unto us, If a man's brother die, and leave his wife behind him, and leave no children, that his brother should take his wife, and raise up seed unto his brother.

20 Now there were seven brethren: and the first took a wife, and dying left no seed.

21 And the second took her, and died, neither left he any seed: and the third likewise.

22 And the seven had her, and left no seed: last of all the woman died also.

I'm sure there are books written solely about seeds. There is so much to this revelation that I could write continuously! However, I do want to point out that our seed (offspring) pays for our sins and they receive the rewards if we leave blessings. So, we desire that God fill us with the strength to leave blessings to our children for our obedience.

Spiritual Seeds

Jesus spoke a parable to the Pharisees and Sadducees about seeds. You can find this in three books of the Gospels; in Luke 8, Matthew 13 and Mark 4. Let's start by reading Mark 4:26:

Mark 4::3-8, 13-15, 26

3 Hearken; Behold, there went out a sower to sow:

4 And it came to pass, as he sowed, some fell by the way side, and the fowls of the air came and devoured it up.

5 And some fell on stony ground, where it had not much earth; and immediately it sprang up, because it had no depth of earth:

6 But when the sun was up, it was scorched; and because it had no root, it withered away.

7 And some fell among thorns, and the thorns grew up, and choked it, and it yielded no fruit.

---

8 And other fell on good ground, and did yield fruit that sprang up and increased; and brought forth, some thirty, and some sixty, and some an hundred.

13 And he said unto them, Know ye not this parable? and how then will ye know all parables?

14 The sower soweth the word.

15 And these are they by the way side, where the word is sown; but when they have heard, Satan cometh immediately, and taketh away the word that was sown in their hearts.

26 And he said, So is the kingdom of God, as if a man should cast seed into the ground;

Mark 13:19 When any one heareth the word of the kingdom, and understandeth it not, then cometh the wicked one, and catcheth away that which was sown in his heart. This is he which received seed by the way side.

As you can see by this parable, the spiritual seeds are significant and we must not discard them easily. Please notice about the soil in which the seeds were attached to and result thereof. God wants us to keep our soil rich and clean.

How Trees Release and Receive Seeds

As a tree in God's great garden, we must be careful in how we receive seeds (pollination) +from other trees or our surroundings.

Mark 4:26 - And he said, So is the kingdom of God, as if a man should cast seed into the ground;

Mouth Seeds

When we speak, we release audible voice seeds. Just imagine if you tell an little eight (8) year-old girl, "You are so ugly." That audible voice word curse seed just then planted within that child will then grow and may result in her growing up as a very sad tree.

She may always feel ugly because of that one seed, planted deep within her soul (mind, will and emotions) and spirit being.

It's the same concept when we are witnessing to people. We are only required to plant seeds. God will water those seeds and produce His harvest.

We should never take glory when someone gets saved, or a manifestation happens from the Holy Ghost because many other people probably planted seeds into that person, and the Holy Spirit just watered it. We are all just conduits for His glory. We just plant and release seeds how, when and where He tells us.

The Bible says LIFE and death is in the power of our tongue. We use our members, the tongue, to release seeds to give LIFE to other people. We can also release death seeds such as the example earlier with the eight-year-old girl. LIFE seeds produce good fruit and more LIFE. DEATH seeds produce bad fruit and more DEATH. We must be careful to use our tongues to release LIFE and good fruit in others.

The Bible also talks about seeds in our Earthly and Heavenly family genealogy. Look at this:

Galatians 3:29 – (KJV) - And if ye be Christ's, then are ye Abraham's seed, and heirs according to the promise.

He also promises us that our seed will be saved:

> *Acts 16:31 – And they said, Believe on the Lord Jesus Christ, and thou shalt be saved, and thy house.*

Eye Seeds

Basically there are many ways to release seeds. You can have sight seeds. If you look at someone with lust in your eyes, then you are sowing lust into them if they receive that seed. Think about how looks and the way you see things communicate to others. They are implanting seeds. If I were to wear a revealing blouse it will impart seeds of lust to anyone who may want to receive that seed. If that seed is not immediately rejected, it may begin to take root.

For example, I had someone show me a picture of a lustful nature and that picture bothered me for days. I had a lustful dream, etc. All I did was glance at it! It was an accident I even saw it. However, because it entered my tree through the eye-gate, then it started to take root until I caught on to it and prayed it out. I repented that the image came before my eyes. I believe this is why the enemy bombards us with horrible and lustful images. It is to taint our tree and temple.

Hand Seeds

My touch may be another seed. When I hug someone, it provides feelings of love and acceptance. Just the gentle touch can impart many seeds of love and good will. However, a person that touches you inappropriately can impart seeds in a bad way.

Those seeds can also take root.

I long to travel to the nations and touch the faces of the nations.

I asked the Lord to allow me to travel and touch all the faces of the nations of the Earth before He takes me home.

This is a dream because I am a passionate person and I want to feel with my hands the creation of God. I want them to feel the genuine love through my hands and respect for their culture. I am the type that I love and respect all cultures. I may not participate in witchcraft activities, etc., but I will respect it. So, touching will be a way to release a seed to those nations that may not understand my language.

Also, when we discuss the touching, I think of this scripture:

> *2 Corinthians 6:17 - Wherefore come out from among them, and be ye separate, saith the Lord, and touch not the unclean thing; and I will receive you,*

Touch not the unclean thing means to avoid the worldly pleasures. It is touching things that the spirit of antichrist birthed into the world. I think about Smith Wigglesworth and how he wouldn't allow Lester Sumrall to come into his house with a worldly newspaper. He protected his home from outside appearances and influences.

It is the Bride separating herself from worldly things. We avoid the very appearance of evil.

> *Isaiah 52:11 - Depart ye, depart ye, go ye out from thence, touch no unclean thing; go ye out of the midst of her; be ye clean, that bear the vessels of the LORD.*

Ear Seeds

The ear and hearing seeds are what we are allowing to come in our tree. If we allow seeds of destruction to come in through your ear-gate, then it will impart those seeds.

The Lord convicted me over my love of Hip-Hop music and coaching cheerleading. I taught all those little girls dance routines based upon that ungodly, demonic music. I imparted the seeds of this music into those other trees.

When you hear a song about lusting or sex, it will impart seeds into your tree. They will uproot one day unless you cut that root off and release those seeds from your tree. We must protect what enters our ears and protect our tree from those seeds entering in.

Nose Seeds

The smelling reflects on the nose and what we allow in imparts seeds. It also means discernment. We should be able to recognize good and evil through smells. Look at this scripture:

2 Corinthians 2:14-17

14 Now thanks be unto God, which always causeth us to triumph in Christ, and maketh manifest the savour of his knowledge by us in every place.

15 For we are unto God a sweet savour of Christ, in them that are saved, and in them that perish:

16 To the one we are the savour of death unto death; and to the other the savour of life unto life. And who is sufficient for these things?

> *17 For we are not as many, which corrupt the word of God: but as of sincerity, but as of God, in the sight of God speak we in Christ.*

We can sense when something evil is around or when God enters the room. There is a fragrance around God that is indescribable. I experienced the smell of God one time:

I was driving to Florida on my way to a women's conference in 2015 and God filled my car with His presence and aroma. It was so amazing that I kept taking in deep breaths and couldn't get enough of Him. His smell was so beautiful! I cannot put it into words. I tell the rest of this story later on in the book.

Then I think of God having bowls of the incense of our prayers around Him and how He loves to smell our prayers. How neat is that? Look at this:

Revelation 5:1-14

1 And I saw in the right hand of him that sat on the throne a book written within and on the backside, sealed with seven seals.

2 And I saw a strong angel proclaiming with a loud voice, Who is worthy to open the book, and to loose the seals thereof? 3 And no man in heaven, nor in earth, neither under the earth, was able to open the book, neither to look thereon.

4 And I wept much, because no man was found worthy to open and to read the book, neither to look thereon.

5 And one of the elders saith unto me, Weep not:

115

behold, the Lion of the tribe of Judah, the Root of David, hath prevailed to open the book, and to loose the seven seals thereof.

6 And I beheld, and, lo, in the midst of the throne and of the four beasts, and in the midst of the elders, stood a Lamb as it had been slain, having seven horns and seven eyes, which are the seven Spirits of God sent forth into all the earth.

7 And he came and took the book out of the right hand of him that sat upon the throne.

8 And when he had taken the book, the four beasts and four and twenty elders fell down before the Lamb, having every one of them harps, and golden vials full of odours, which are the prayers of saints.

9 And they sung a new song, saying, Thou art worthy to take the book, and to open the seals thereof: for thou wast slain, and hast redeemed us to God by thy blood out of every kindred, and tongue, and people, and nation;

10 And hast made us unto our God kings and priests: and we shall reign on the earth.

11 And I beheld, and I heard the voice of many angels round about the throne and the beasts and the elders: and the number of them was ten thousand times ten thousand, and thousands of thousands;

12 Saying with a loud voice, Worthy is the Lamb

that was slain to receive power, and riches, and wisdom, and strength, and honour, and glory, and blessing.

13 And every creature which is in heaven, and on the earth, and under the earth, and such as are in the sea, and all that are in them, heard I saying, Blessing, and honour, and glory, and power, be unto him that sitteth upon the throne, and unto the Lamb for ever and ever.

14 And the four beasts said, Amen. And the four and twenty elders fell down and worshipped him that liveth for ever and ever.

The angels were holding the bowls of incense which are the prayers of the saints. Isn't that awesome to know that God gathers the prayers and smells them? Look at this:

Hebrews 5:14 - But strong meat belongeth to them that are of full age, even those who by reason of use have their senses exercised to discern both good and evil.

We need to pray that God increases our senses so that we can know good and evil by smell and other senses. One other example of evil smells is death. Death can have a foul odor. Look at this:

Amos 4:10 - "I sent a plague among you after the manner of Egypt; I slew your young men by the sword along with your captured horses, And I made the stench of your camp rise up in your nostrils; Yet you have not returned to Me," declares the LORD.

While we're on smells and odors, I want to point out that Jesus' sacrifice for us was a scent to God and thus when we are in Christ, we become a great smell to God. Look at this:

> *Ephesians 5:2 and walk in love, just as Christ also loved you and gave Himself up for us, an offering and a sacrifice to God as a fragrant aroma.*
>
> *2 Corinthians 2:14-16*
>
> *14 Now thanks be unto God, which always causeth us to triumph in Christ, and maketh manifest the savour of his knowledge by us in every place.*
>
> *15 For we are unto God a sweet savour of Christ, in them that are saved, and in them that perish:*
>
> *16 To the one we are the savour of death unto death; and to the other the savour of life unto life. And who is sufficient for these things?*

Bride, we must protect all the seeds that enter and exit.

9

GUARD THE GATES
TO THE GARDEN

There are many teachings out there about gates; however, the gates I present in this book are from my revelation from God. Please pray and ask Him to reveal this to you.

So far we have discussed the five-fold senses and how it imparts seeds.

1. The Vision (eyes)

2. The Hearing (ears)

3. The Touching (hands)

4. The Tasting (mouth)

5. The Smelling (nose)

Due to the revelation about the seeds, we must block seeds from entering our tree by protecting the garden and gates. You know the old saying, "What comes in will come out." Now that we discussed the way we can pass seeds from tree to tree or from environment to our trees, we must protect the gates into our tree:

1. Eye Gate

2. Ear Gate

3. Mouth Gate

4. Hand Gate

5. Sexual Gate

6. Heart Gate

Each one of these gates will allow things in and if we're not careful it will express itself through an exit out of the tree, or an action of sin/disobedience to God.

Sexual Gate

I'm going to start with the sexual gate because the spirit of antichrist is deceiving so many people in this area. I know because I was deceived greatly in this area.

We all know that the Bible describes marriage as the institution between one man and one woman. God created sex for this institution.

> *Genesis 1:28-29 - God created man in His image; in the Divine image he created him; male and female He created them. God blessed them, saying: "Be fertile and multiply; fill the earth and subdue it."*

It is something to be enjoyed in the right environment. For instance, the Bible says that the marriage bed is undefiled.

> *Hebrews 13:4 - Marriage is honorable in all, and the bed undefiled: but whoremongers and adulterers God will judge.*

This means that God meant for husband and wife to enjoy the marriage bed. Satan destroys this image of perfect unity between a man and woman and attempts to defile it.

The ultimate defilement is homosexuality. The reason it is so impure is because it goes against nature itself. This means it goes against the whole purpose of God creating mankind.

According to this scripture reference, the ones who open themselves up to homosexuality also open themselves up to a whole pack of demons. Check this out on what attaches itself to this seed:

Romans 1:26-32

26 For this cause God gave them up unto vile affections: for even their women did change the natural use into that which is against nature:

27 And likewise also the men, leaving the natural use of the woman, burned in their lust one toward another; men with men working that which is unseemly, and receiving in themselves that recompense of their error which was meet.

28 And even as they did not like to retain God in their knowledge, God gave them over to a reprobate mind, to do those things which are not convenient;

29 Being filled with all unrighteousness, fornication, wickedness, covetousness, maliciousness; full of envy, murder, debate, deceit, malignity; whisperers,

30 Backbiters, haters of God, despiteful, proud, boasters, inventors of evil things, disobedient to parents,

31 Without understanding, covenant breakers, without natural affection, implacable, unmerciful:

32 Who knowing the judgment of God, that they which commit such things are worthy of death, not only do the same, but have pleasure in them that do them.

The Bible talks about the impact having sex outside of the marriage confines within God's blessing:

1 Corinthians 6 15-20

15 Know ye not that your bodies are the members of Christ? shall I then take the members of Christ, and make them the members of an harlot? God forbid.

16 What? know ye not that he which is joined to an harlot is one body? for two, saith he, shall be one flesh.

17 But he that is joined unto the Lord is one spirit.

18 Flee fornication. Every sin that a man doeth is without the body; but he that committeth fornication sinneth against his own body.

19 What? know ye not that your body is the temple of the Holy Ghost which is in you, which ye have of God, and ye are not your own?

20 For ye are bought with a price: therefore glorify God in your body, and in your spirit, which are God's.

When you open your tree up to the sexual gate, you are opening it up to the other tree's demons and seeds. They enter your tree and take root. All the seeds I mention in this book, if we do not remove them from our tree, then they will take root and sprout up sometime in our lives.

I pray you understand a little about the Sexual Gate. God only means it to be within the confines of marriage. Thus, it should be closed.

This is the gate where the seed is released from the man (husband) into the woman (wife) to impregnate her with life. This seed produces life and is holy before God. God then releases a spirit from Heaven to Earth. In the end, all spirits return to God.

> *Ecclesiastes 12:7 - Then shall the dust return to the earth as it was: and the spirit shall return unto God who gave it.*

The Mouth Gate

This is the hardest gate to keep closed. The Bible says it is an unruly member. It also says that we can speak life or death. I talk about this a lot when I discussed the audible seeds, but I do need to reflect on the gate of the mouth.

> *Proverbs 18:21 - Death and life are in the power of the tongue: and they that love it shall eat the fruit thereof.*

I found this powerful teaching about words:

Our words carry power. They are spiritual seeds, which we "plant" to bring forth a harvest of one type or another. I'm not just talking about our words of prayer, but whatever words we use. Everything we do in the spirit realm is through our words.

123

We pray with words, we worship with words, we break curses with words, we cast out demons with words, and we bless with words. Every word we speak enters the spirit realm and causes some effect. (Murphy, 2004)

Through this gate, if we're not careful, we can allow demonic activity to be released into our lives. If we speak death and curses over ourselves, we grant the enemy permission to wreak havoc over our lives. Example:

One day, Jesus and His disciples were walking from Bethany to Jerusalem. Jesus was hungry, and decided to eat. Unfortunately, the fig tree that He wanted to eat from didn't have any fruit on it, so He cursed it.

> *Mark 11:13-14*
>
> *13 And seeing a fig tree afar off having leaves, he came, if haply he might find anything thereon: and when he came to it, he found nothing but leaves; for the time of figs was not yet.*
>
> *14 And Jesus answered and said unto it, No man eat fruit of thee hereafter forever. And his disciples heard it.*
>
> *Mark 11:20 - And in the morning, as they passed by, they saw the fig tree dried up from the roots.*

What happened to the tree? The force of the curse that Jesus spoke forth took hold of that tree and killed it. Had He spoken a blessing over it, the tree would have been blessed. But, since He spoke a curse over it, it died. *(Murphy, 2004)*

As I said previously, what comes in will come out. **What releases out of our mouth; we will answer on Judgment Day.**

Matthew 12: 33-37

33 Either make the tree good, and his fruit good; or else make the tree corrupt, and his fruit corrupt: for the tree is known by his fruit.

34 O generation of vipers, how can ye, being evil, speak good things? for out of the abundance of the heart the mouth speaketh.

35 A good man out of the good treasure of the heart bringeth forth good things: and an evil man out of the evil treasure bringeth forth evil things.

36 But I say unto you, That every idle word that men shall speak, they shall give account thereof in the day of judgment.

37 For by thy words thou shalt be justified, and by thy words thou shalt be condemned.

This can be compared to the audible seeds as well.

As far as being held accountable for what enters our body through the mouth gate, we are not warned against this:

Matthew 15:11 - Not that which goeth into the mouth defileth a man; but that which cometh out of the mouth, this defileth a man.

Needless to say, our mouth can be a lethal weapon. It can slice and dice a human without any other weapon.

I would like to add one more way to use our mouth gate for God's glory is smiling. Did you know a smile can make someone's day? A smile can literally change the mood for someone who is depressed or hurting.

> **Proverbs 15:13, 30**
>
> **13 - A glad heart makes a happy face: a broken heart crushes the spirit.**
>
> **30 – A friendly smile makes you happy and good news makes you feel strong.**

Please notice how the first scripture says the heart can change the face. Also on the second verse it says if we change the face it changes the heart. Interesting.

The Ear Gate

Like I said earlier about the music, it is basically what we are allowing into our tree through this gate. Also, think about hearing bad news. Once we hear it, we must figure it out within ourselves what to do with that information. Sometimes we say, "I wish you wouldn't have told me. I wish I didn't know this or that." The reason we say that is because now it is a seed and we must decide what to do about that seed.

If we are not careful we will make the wrong decision. When I was partying and listening to that Hip-Hop sexual music, I could listen to certain songs when I was "in the mood". I knew those songs could take me where I wanted to go. Now that I have surrendered my tree to the creator, I reject those types of songs and fill my tree with holy and pure songs. I know what songs cause me to romance my husband (Jesus).

I know what songs will take me into the throne room of worship. Music is a power.

In addition to music and the outer influences, we must consider what we hear. There is a difference between listening and hearing.

I can listen to worldly music in a grocery store, but I may not be hearing it. I may tune it out amongst the other noise in the room. This is why the Bible says, "Let you hear what the spirit is saying to the churches". It says this because it wants you to really listen and pay attention to what God is saying. It means that we have our full focus and attention on those words that we are hearing.

We must tune-out the noise and distractions and hear the spirit of the Lord for our temples. He wants our full attention. We need to understand what the spirit is trying to relay to us.

Isn't it interesting that faith comes by hearing and hearing by the word of God. Look at this scripture:

> **Romans 10:17 – So then faith comes by hearing, and hearing by the word of God.**

Faith comes by hearing means when we hear what God is saying through His word, not just listening to it, then we will receive His words and it will build our faith. This means that we are focuses on what He is saying. We have understanding of it and we receive it.

Hearing by the word of God means that the word of God is going to speak to us. His word does not return void. His words are life.

Look at this:

> *Hebrews 4:12 – For the word of God is quick and powerful, and sharper than any two-edged sword, piercing even to dividing asunder of soul and spirit, and joints and marrow, and is a discerner of the thoughts and intents of the heart.*

So, when we are hearing the word of God, it is examining our heart, piercing our soul and cleaning our hearts. The Bible says that the Holy Spirit is the searcher of man's hearts. It also says that the word of God is a mirror where we must face our self. The word is like an X-ray machine.

The Eye Gate

The eye gate is a way for our souls to reach out to the outside world. We look at things and ponder on them. We see things and consider them. What we see can bring seeds in, and then we must decide whether to bury the seed, act on the seed, or discard the seed. We may ask God to forgive us for what we saw. We may decide to act upon what we saw. We may decide to think about it later or dismiss it. However, what come in is buried in the tree somewhere.

Consider how they do with what we've seen in movies with mentally insane people sitting in a chair and them flashing images into their eyes. These images are horror pictures, terrorizing images, etc. It can drive someone mad when they see such devastating images. It can also make a person tolerant of something because they have seen so much of the seed that it is planted in them and has built a root.

The Bible talks about the lust of the eyes causing us much grief:

I also consider Eve when she ate of the fruit. She saw that it was good and took it. She lusted after that fruit, thus she acted on it.

The Hand Gate

The hand gate is a powerful gate in that through the hands people are delivered, healed and set free. God commands us to lay hands on people. There must be a reason that it's through the hands. Look at this:

Mark 16:17-18

17 And these signs will follow those who believe: In My name they will cast out demons; they will speak with new tongues;

18 they[a] will take up serpents; and if they drink anything deadly, it will by no means hurt them; they will lay hands on the sick, and they will recover."

There is an impartation that takes place through hands. I was asking God how this happens. He reminded me that He is the vine, and we are the branches. Our hands represent His branches reaching out to humanity.

The Bible also states to lay hands suddenly on no man. This can be interpreted many ways. One way meaning that what they have can come back to you and enter into you.

Another way means that we are to be slow to anger and withhold our hands in reaction to someone or a situation. The other way it means we are to be very careful and treasure the anointing on the inside of us and do not be sudden or rash about releasing that to just anyone. Either way, be careful about laying your hands on someone.

Hands are also used in a weapon of war. Your hands are a battlefield in the spirit. We lift our hands to praise God.

Psalm 144:1 - Blessed be the Lord my strength which teacheth my hands to war, and my fingers to fight:

This can also mean in the spirit. Our hands waving in the air is like waving palm branches of worship and offering in the air. The Bible says that the trees of the field they clap their hands. I believe that is us!

Heart Gate

The enemy tries to come in through our emotions. The Bible says the heart is deceitful, thus we cannot trust it. We must trust His word over our heart any day! We will want to do something because we have the heart or compassion for someone or something, but if God didn't tell you to do it, etc., then it can be a way for the enemy to step in.

The enemy tries to come in through our emotions. The Bible says the heart is deceitful, thus we cannot trust it. We must trust His word over our hearts any day! We may want to do something because we have the heart or compassion for someone or something, but if God doesn't tell you to do it, etc., it can be a way for the enemy to step in.

The main way the enemy comes in through the heart to destroy us is offense. If we accept the offense and not bounce it right back by saying out of our mouth, "I forgive you," it will bury itself within our hearts and forms a root of bitterness. When we have opened that door to offense, we've opened a big gaping wound in our heart through which other sins may enter. We must forgive quickly and not allow it to take root.

Your heart can deceive you into sin as well. I have been confronted by homosexuals who have said, "How can you tell me I can't love someone?" I say, "Well, then is it OK for me to LOVE my son, or LOVE my father or cousin?" Then they say, "No, that is incest." Then, I reply, "Oh, now you're measuring love? Hmmm. How is that different than you loving the same sex? What if I love my dog or horse? What if I want to love it and marry it? I have feelings, and I truly love my animals." See, the heart is deceitful.

Also, the heart may tell us to do something sinful because it wants it. However, we must consider that the heart is reacting out of what we put in there.

> **Proverbs 21:2 – Every way of a man is right in his own eyes: but the Lord pondereth the hearts.**

So, what if I fell in love with a married man based off of my loneliness or based off the lust I've allowed in?

I'm opening the door to sin. I could say, "But I love him." The truth is, you can choose to leave that situation and not go down that road.

It is also true that what we allow to come in will come out when we are under pressure. Just pressure someone, and see what comes out. If he curses, it's because of what is in his heart. We also may witness anger rising up real quickly when he has unresolved bitterness. Look at this scripture:

> *Luke 6:45 A good man out of the good treasure of his heart bringeth forth that which is good; and an evil man out of the evil treasure of his heart bringeth forth that which is evil: for of the abundance of the heart his mouth speaketh.*

Please reflect as well on the dream I wrote about earlier in this chapter about the big fluffy pretty tree in the forest and the arrows of offense flying towards it.

The difference is his reaction to the arrows. We must guard our hearts to keep evil out, and walk in forgiveness.

Forgiveness of the Heart

I must write about forgiveness because of the troubling times the Bride is entering into. Please pay attention to the enemy's tactics.

I studied media during graduate school, and I know how the media is run by a certain few. Some would argue that the Illuminati are the ones who control the gates of what comes into the mainstream news, television shows, movies, music, etc.

If you want to know more, read my book, *Selling the Mark of the Beast, Marketing RFID, EU vs. US*. It is about my trip to London in December 2011 through January 2012.

I discovered that they are chipping people today in Europe and the United States.

One thing for sure is that the spirit of antichrist is ruling the Earth, and it wants to instill anger in our hearts. The media purposefully shows us images and video to spark the reactions that they desire.

They may want Christians to let down their guard or to act a certain way to prepare them for their global agenda to chip all humans with an RFID (radio frequency identification device) tag. Some may argue that is the mark of the beast. So, how will they brainwash society to take this chip? They will just continue to show us scary situations like ISIS killing Christians. One of the purposes is to instill anger in our hearts towards that group and others. Please bear with me a minute as I explain.

If we watch this and allow it to take root in our hearts, when they come to our door to kill us or torture us, what will come out of our hearts? Of course, it will be anger. God does not want that to happen. He wants us to forgive and love. It's hard to love when we are full of bitterness. Those are seeds that Satan wants to put in your temple. Shut that door so the seed cannot enter.

When you see situations like that on television, say in your heart, "I forgive them Lord." People do not realize that unforgiveness roots can come through the visual even though it may not be directly addressing them. It is what you see through the eye gate. I'm also addressing this as a way to enter the heart gate as well. We want to be like Stephen in the Bible where we will be full of God's love towards that person or people. We must love them until the death. I have some friends that travel to Egypt and they say this is how Muslims are being converted is forgiveness!

Protect your heart and walk in forgiveness. Unforgiveness builds hard roots and will clog up your relationship with God.

It will cause sickness and other things. It's not worth it. Forgive.

Pastor Carolyn Sissom
Eastgate Church, Katy, TX
The Enemy; The Fox

Beware Christians of the enemy who comes in like a sly fox to spoil the vine and to steal your seeds. Carolyn Sissom, Pastor or Eastgate Church in Texas, wrote in her latest newsletter;

Song 2:15: "...the little foxes spoil the vines..."

Whether in marriage, friendship or church fellowship, it is the little foxes who spoil the vines.

The foxes are things that hinder. They abort the seed. These foxes sneak in under the leaves. These have affinity with the serpents, and are known for their craftiness, especially in playing dead. They were mentioned by Ezekiel to be false prophets (including false words of condemnation – Prov. 17:15.) It is those little insignificant things that we have allowed to feed unmolested among our vines. These habits, words, or weaknesses (which appear as nothing in themselves) are deceitful and cute, treacherous and sly: wasted time, foolish talking, lack of diligence, neglect of prayer. The fruit of life is full of promise. If unwatched or unguarded now, the little things can ruin it all.

All criticism, condemnation, naysayers, negative talk, unkindness, gossip, tale-bearing, stirring of strife, false judgments, etc. are the voices of false prophets. How do I know they are false prophets? Because, those voices are never from God.

When the Lord corrects us, he does so with truth. "You shall know the truth and the truth shall set you free." God's truth will not be a dagger.

It will have the effect of liberating us from our pain and our hurt. (Sissom, 2016)

This is why we need a great cloud of witnesses around us. We need mentors and people who will keep their spiritual eyes open over our souls. They are watchmen on the wall. The enemy can't get through the gates because you're surrounded by protection. Our problem becomes when we do not want to hear from the wise counsel or we manipulate the wise counsel to achieve our goals.

When we surrender ourselves to our inner circle, and are truthful with them, we are protected by other eyes to guard our souls from the foxes. Only pride will keep us from accepting wisdom, criticism, instruction and rebuke. When we get to that place, we're basically backslidden because pride has raised its ugly head. We must stay humble and transparent before others so that the foxes are exposed. If we go through that door with pride as the key, the enemy is just waiting on the other side to destroy. Keep the gates closed, Bride. Trust those you have entrusted with your life.

I must end the chapter about the gates with this song we all sang as a child in Sunday school:

Oh Be Careful Little Eyes

O be careful little eyes what you see
O be careful little eyes what you see
There's a Father up above
And He's looking down in love
So, be careful little eyes what you see

O be careful little ears what you hear
O be careful little ears what you hear

There's a Father up above
And He's looking down in love
So, be careful little ears what you hear

O be careful little hands what you do
O be careful little hands what you do
There's a Father up above
And He's looking down in love
So, be careful little hands what you do
Oh Be Careful Little Eyes Cont'd

O be careful little feet where you go
O be careful little feet where you go
There's a Father up above
And He's looking down in love
So, be careful little feet where you go

O be careful little mouth what you say
O be careful little mouth what you say
There's a Father up above
And He's looking down in love
So, be careful little mouth what you say
(Child Bible Songs)

10

JESUS & THE GARDEN

Jesus willingly left His kingdom and entered our sin-ridden kingdom. He chose to DIE ON A TREE as our sacrificial Lamb to bring God's life-giving breath back to us once again. Today we no longer have to sacrifice animals to God to have our sins covered because Jesus has already covered our sins with His precious blood, which is our atonement. Praise God!

When we accept Jesus Christ into our hearts and lives to SAVE and REDEEM US from the Adamic Curse and the Curse of the Law, His precious blood is applied to our past sins. We are forgiven, and we enter into the family and garden of God.

So, when it came time for Jesus to die on the cross, He willingly took on all the sins of humanity on his person as He was the perfect Lamb who was slain.

John 1:29 - "Here is the Lamb of God who takes away the sin of the world."

When Jesus came, He reconnected us to the Vine and the Rivers of Living Water! Now, we have full access to God as in the Garden of Eden! God looks at us like a garden, just as the Bible book, Song of Solomon, talks about God's love for us!

When Jesus died on the cross, He became one with His Bride! They nailed Him to a TREE! Some theorize that he hung on a tree. The undisputable fact is that He bled on a tree.

When He suffered on that tree, blood was passed from Jesus to the tree. This is the covenant that Jesus makes with His Bride.

At that moment, we became one with our husband. This is how Jesus married us, in that He laid down His life for us. As I'm finishing this book today, it is Good Friday 2016. What a prophetic significance to releasing this book in two days on Easter! He shed His blood for us Bride so that we have access back into the garden and relationship with our Creator!

In order for us to be the True Bride, we must lay down our lives (hopes and dreams) for Him. We must die to SELF!

God nourishes our trees through the word and His presence. God wants to talk to us like we can talk to plants. Studies have shown that plants grow better by humans talking and encouraging them.

God's son, Jesus, is the Light of God which shines on us for our spiritual growth. The more we are in Jesus' presence; the more we are transformed from our natural, carnal man into the man God has ordained. When Jesus was hanging on the cross, God had to turn away because He cannot look upon sin. Jesus is sometimes referred to the as Vine in the scriptures. When He was in the garden and in prayer before He was crucified, He was pressured and was praying so hard that his sweat began to turn to blood. The wine was being pressed in the wine garden.

Israel was God's Bride

In the Old Testament, God mentions many times how Israel was His Bride. He mentions it like the people are one in His eyes. Here are a few examples:

Jeremiah 3:8 – And I saw when for all the causes whereby backsliding Israel committed adultery I had put her away, and given her a bill of divorce; yet her treacherous sister Judah feared not, but went and played the harlot also.

Jeremiah 3:14-20

14 "Return, O backsliding children," says the Lord; "for I am married to you. I will take you, one from a city and two from a family, and I will bring you to Zion.

15 And I will give you shepherds according to My heart, who will feed you with knowledge and understanding.

16 "Then it shall come to pass, when you are multiplied and increased in the land in those days," says the Lord, "that they will say no more, 'The ark of the covenant of the Lord.' It shall not come to mind, nor shall they remember it, nor shall they visit it, nor shall it be made anymore.

17 "At that time Jerusalem shall be called The Throne of the Lord, and all the nations shall be gathered to it, to the name of the Lord, to Jerusalem. No more shall they follow the dictates of their evil hearts.

18 "In those days the house of Judah shall walk with the house of Israel, and they shall come together out of the land of the north to the land that I have given as an inheritance to your fathers.

19 "But I said: 'How can I put you among the children And give you a pleasant land, A beautiful heritage of the hosts of nations?' "And I said: 'You shall call Me, "My Father," And not turn away from Me.'

20 Surely, as a wife treacherously departs from her husband, So have you dealt treacherously with Me, O house of Israel," says the Lord.

Needless to say, God had many battles with Israel by her cheating on Him, serving other idols, etc. But, He never gave up on her, and sometimes He had to whip her a little to draw her back to Him.

Whenever the Bride would get off course, He would allow her to go off in her sin and reap the consequences of it (being held captive by the enemy, etc.). Following this discipline, the Bride would always turn back to God and repent. We are about to see this with America. America's founding fathers made a covenant with God on this land, and we have turned our backs on Him just like Israel did. We will have to suffer the consequences so that His people can return to Him in repentance. He is jealous for us!

Also remember how I explained earlier that when we sin, it opens the door for the enemy in our lives, it is the same way for America. We opened the door, thus God has to pull back because we hurt Him. He cannot reside where we do not honor Him. Woe to America when His hand is removed even the slightest! Remember that dome? We will no longer be under that protection of the Almighty! I talk about this in the *Clarion Call to UNITY in the Bride of Christ* book.

The Church is Jesus' Bride

Nonetheless, the Old Testament foretold of how Jesus would come and save humanity. This takes place as God comes to Earth and impregnates a human from Israel (Mary), and births a son into the atmosphere (Jesus).

> *Matthew 1:18 – Now the birth of Jesus Christ was on this wise: When as his mother Mary was espoused to Joseph before they came together, she was found with child of the Holy Ghost.*

> *Luke 1:34-35*

> *34 Then Mary said to the angel, "How can this be, since I do not know a man?"*

> *35 And the angel answered and said to her, "The Holy Spirit will come upon you, and the power of the Highest will overshadow you; therefore, also, that Holy One who is to be born will be called the Son of God.*

Jesus already existed before his manifestation on Earth. There are many instances in the Old Testament where Jesus is reflected. However, this scripture best describes Jesus' pre-existence –

> *John 17:5 – And now, O Father, glorify thou me with thine own self with the glory which I had*

141

The Price of Jesus – The Betrothal

In order to redeem mankind from the curse of Adam and Eve, God must provide the perfect sacrifice to atone for sin. He needed something that not only covered the sin but actually redeemed mankind back to the garden-state of relationship. Jesus loved the Church so much that He chose to give up His throne in Heaven and come to Earth in the form of flesh to redeem man back to God. He offered His LIFE as the perfect sacrifice for man's sin.

When Jesus came to Earth, He was born of a virgin mother whom the Holy Spirit had impregnated. When Jesus was born, He had to live a LIFE on Earth as a mortal man and be tempted in all ways as humans. In other words, He had to pass the test.

When Satan took Him up on the mountain to tempt Him, He offered Jesus the world if He would just bow down and worship him (Satan). Jesus used the word against him and overcame the temptation. However, Satan still uses that trick with people today.

Many of the pop-stars and big Hollywood people have sold their souls to the devil for the fortune of fame.

Money is not evil; it's the love of money that is evil.

Yes, God loves His only begotten son, Jesus, more than we love our children. Knowing it was but temporary, it still hurt Father God. He witnessed His only begotten son mocked for being His son, tortured for our healing, bleeding and dying for OUR Salvation. However, God allowed this all to happen to His Jesus because He loves us.

Jesus provides a great parable about this:

Luke 20:9-19

9 Then began he to speak to the people this parable; A certain man planted a vineyard, and let it forth to husbandmen, and went into a far country for a long time.

10 And at the season he sent a servant to the husbandmen, that they should give him of the fruit of the vineyard: but the husbandmen beat him, and sent him away empty.

11 And again he sent another servant: and they beat him also, and entreated him shamefully, and sent him away empty.

12 And again he sent a third: and they wounded him also, and cast him out.

13 Then said the lord of the vineyard, What shall I do? I will send my beloved son: it may be they will reverence him when they see him.

14 But when the husbandmen saw him, they reasoned among themselves, saying, This is the heir: come, let us kill him, that the inheritance may be ours.

15 So they cast him out of the vineyard, and killed him. What therefore shall the lord of the vineyard do unto them?

16 He shall come and destroy these husbandmen, and shall give the vineyard to others. And when they heard it, they said, God forbid.

17 And he beheld them, and said, What is this then that is written, The stone which the builders rejected, the same is become the head of the corner?

18 Whosoever shall fall upon that stone shall be broken; but on whomsoever it shall fall, it will grind him to powder.

19 And the chief priests and the scribes the same hour sought to lay hands on him; and they feared the people: for they perceived that he had spoken this parable against them

The son in this parable is Jesus. This is God's point of view. How do I know this? God gave me a dream, in the midst of a situation.

I was very upset in my heart about leaders mistreating my preacher son. They often rebuked him for hours on end because of his special spiritual gifts. Afterward, I would ask him about it, and he would always say, "It's OK, Momma." He always had love. They treated the other children better than him because they were inferior to his giftings. (I don't know this for sure, but this is how I felt at the time).

He was extremely gifted, and God used him greatly. He was winning his high school for Jesus and conducting a Tuesday night youth prayer gathering in the community. It was normal for about 75 kids each week to be worshipping together in UNITY.

The whole community was greatly changed over a short period of time.

The point is that it hurt me to see people hurting my son. One night I had a dream:

Dream about God Turning His Back on Jesus at Cross

My son, Brock, and I attended a major television minister's meeting in a large stadium. Brock's mentor was the guest speaker. At the end of the meeting, Brock went running toward the stage screaming the television minister's name, "You're my mentor! I love you! I have all your books and listen to all your materials!"

When he made it to the stage and to the minister, he lovingly hugged the television minister. The more he loved him; all of a sudden the minister's face started melting. The television minister seemed to know that he was about to be exposed so he yelled in an angry voice, "Brock! Downstairs now!" So he and Brock disappeared.

I sat in the stadium and waited for hours! I was getting so mad while I was waiting because I knew he was mistreating my son!

Eventually, I turned around, and there was my son. He was severely burned and looking like he had been beaten to a pulp. He looked black and ashy where they had burned him. All I could see was the whites of his eyes. This anger rose up in me, and I said, "Did the television minister do this to you?" Brock replied as he always did, "It's OK, Momma."

He would say it with such love, and that would make me so mad! Even madder, I said it again, "Tell me if he did this to you!" So Brock said it again, "It's OK, Momma!" Well, I got so mad that I started shaking him screaming at the top of my lungs, "You tell me right now if the television minister did this to you!" Brock answered, "Yes, Mom."

I took off running, screaming, "Television minister when I find you, I'm going to kill you! How dare you hurt my son! I'm going to kill you!"

I was running around the stadium until I was running out of breath. I was wearing myself out running to find this man.

When I came around the corner, a light shone down from heaven and made a big circle in front of me. An authorative voice said, "They did it to my son, too!"

It stopped me dead in my tracks. His voice and words pierced my very being and everything within me. With so much pain in my heart and my body trembling, I couldn't hardly stand it, however I answered God, "But God, this is MY SON! I can't stand it when they hurt my son!" God replied, "Why do you think I had to turn my back when He was on the cross?"

> *Matthew 27:46 – "My God, my God, why have thou forsaken me?"*

I fell to my knees and wept. I'm explaining to God how much it hurt me when they hurt my son. I told him I can't take it anymore. I don't like it when people hurt my innocent son's heart. God replied, "June, if you will trust me with your son, I will take care of him. Trust me."

I cried and then said, "Yes Lord, I will trust you." Then I woke up.

So, I know God was hurting while Jesus was suffering on the cross. Sometimes I still have to remind myself of this dream to continually give my children to God and trust God with them.

Going back to the betrothal, Jesus made the choice to die for the Bride. Jesus made the choice to die for the sins of all those people who will believe and receive Jesus as their personal Savior, allowing Him to become the Lord of their lives.

Revivalist Casey Sones revealed, "When Jesus died, He was buried in a garden!" Following this revelation, Dr. Dianna Senkyrik found the scripture those talks about Jesus being laid to rest in the garden.

> *John 19:40-41*
>
> *40 Then took they the body of Jesus, and wound it in linen clothes with the spices, as the manner of the Jews is to bury.*

41 Now in the place where he was crucified there was a garden; and in the garden a new sepulchre, wherein was never man yet laid.

Symbolism of Jesus Buried in Garden

When Jesus was buried, they placed Him in a garden within a tomb. Outside of the tomb were two angels above the big stone that was rolled to cover the tomb's entrance. The angels were there to prevent anyone from going into the tomb and bothering Jesus' body. This is symbolic as to the angels who were blocking the Garden of Eden. They prevented anyone from entering that place. The angels blocked human's access back into the garden. Sin drove us out. Sin removed us from God's presence. We were barred from entering that holy place again.

The significance of Jesus dying on the cross and bearing our sins upon His being and paying the price for what His Bride did was the ultimate price for love. He gave all. They laid Him to rest in the tomb then as He was in the grave for three days; He went to Hell and retrieved the keys from Satan to death, Hell and the grave. This ensures us that death no longer has a hold on us. Oh the power of what He did! ::gasp::

Just imagine how our King faced Lucifer and said, "Let go of my Bride! You cannot touch her anymore! She is mine and if you want to touch her again, you must go through me!" (My interpretation). Look at this:

Acts 2:24 - Whom God hath raised up, having loosed the pains of death: because it was not possible that he should be holden of it.

Acts 2:31 - He seeing this before spake of the resurrection of Christ, that his soul was not left in hell, neither his flesh did see corruption.

Ephesians 4:8-10

8 Wherefore he saith, When he ascended up on high, he led captivity captive, and gave gifts unto men.

9 (Now that he ascended, what is it but that he also descended first into the lower parts of the earth?

10 He that descended is the same also that ascended up far above all heavens, that he might fill all things.)

Jesus as Sacrifice for Us

According to Jewish culture, for a man to ask a woman to marry him, he must first approach the woman's father and offer a dowry that is suitable for that woman's hand in marriage? It's up to the father as to whether that gift is acceptable for his family or not.

It is the same principal with God and Jesus. Jesus became the perfect sacrificial dowry for the Bride, acceptable to God. This sacrificial dowry of Jesus redeemed the Church once and for all. We now have free access to God because of the Lamb that was slain. At the end of time, it is this Lamb who will break open the seals for God's judgments to be poured out on the Earth. He is the only one worthy to open the seals.

THE PRICE OF MAN – THE ACCEPTANCE

We know what Jesus did to receive us as His Bride. He laid down His LIFE for us. He gave His all. He gave up His Kingdom for us.

Now that we know Jesus' LIFE is acceptable to God as a dowry for the Bride, what will it cost the Bride to marry Jesus?

The Bride of Christ is the Church. It is humanity. Jesus came to redeem and restore man back into a right relationship with God. The Bride is described in scripture as:

> *Isaiah 54:5 – For thy maker is thy husband; the Lord of Hosts is his name; and thy redeemer the Holy One of Israel; The God of the whole earth shall he be called.*

> *Ephesians 5:27 – Husbands love your wives even as Christ also loves the church and gave himself for it.*

The Bride lays down her LIFE for her husband as He did for her. She surrenders all and makes a choice to take on His identity. It all comes from a choice. However, she knows that to marry her King, she must become one with Him in her heart as well as her body.

She loves Him so much that laying her LIFE down for Him is an honor as a living sacrifice, too.

When you love someone you want to please them with all your heart, mind, and soul; ensuring they are pleased with your heart and actions.

As the Bride, we long to please our King at all times. So, laying it down; our hopes, wants, and desires to become one with Him are top priority.

We are willing to allow God to shape, correct, mold, and make us into the perfect Bride that He so desires. We keep our hearts humble and soft before the throne.

When He corrects us or disciplines us, we are thankful as His children. We know that we need much work in order to be in the position to take authority on Earth and to fulfill our destiny.

The Bible says that faith pleases God. As one walks out His destiny on Earth, it requires great faith.

As we keep our hearts before the throne in worship and prayer and read the word of God, God will keep us as a beautiful Bride for His Son.

Revelation about Time

Time is a funny thing. It began when God created the heavens and the Earth. This is the point when measurement began. Time is for a reason. We are only gifted with a certain amount of it, and we must make it count.

Time can either be our best friend or our worst enemy. We can live life like we have all the time in the world and waste it. One day we will find out we did not live the life that God designed for us. Thus, when we stand before Him on Judgment Day, we will answer for that. On the other hand, when we realize what short amount of time we have on Earth, we will live every day knowing that God is the one who blessed us with that time.

We can be snuffed out at any moment! So, we live and embrace today knowing who holds our tomorrow. We do not worry about tomorrow because we are obeying Him today.

When we stand before the throne, we will be rewarded for using our time wisely on Earth. Look at this:

Psalm 18:20-36

20 The Lord rewarded me according to my righteousness; according to the cleanness of my hands hath he recompensed me.

21 For I have kept the ways of the Lord, and have not wickedly departed from my God.

22 For all his judgments were before me, and I did not put away his statutes from me.

23 I was also upright before him, and I kept myself from mine iniquity.

24 Therefore hath the Lord recompensed me according to my righteousness, according to the cleanness of my hands in his eyesight.

25 With the merciful thou wilt shew thyself merciful; with an upright man thou wilt shew thyself upright;

26 With the pure thou wilt shew thyself pure; and with the froward thou wilt shew thyself froward.

27 For thou wilt save the afflicted people; but wilt bring down high looks.

28 For thou wilt light my candle: the Lord my God will enlighten my darkness.

29 For by thee I have run through a troop; and by my God have I leaped over a wall.

30 As for God, his way is perfect: the word of the Lord is tried: he is a buckler to all those that trust in him.

31 For who is God save the Lord? or who is a rock save our God?

32 It is God that girdeth me with strength, and maketh my way perfect.

33 He maketh my feet like hinds' feet, and setteth me upon my high places.

34 He teacheth my hands to war, so that a bow of steel is broken by mine arms.

35 Thou hast also given me the shield of thy salvation: and thy right hand hath holden me up, and thy gentleness hath made me great.

36 Thou hast enlarged my steps under me, that my feet did not slip.

When I discovered the reality of living for today and not worrying about tomorrow, I really began to live. Now I see the birds and the slower time. I wake up every morning thanking the Lord for the opportunity to have another day.

It's really sad when you see someone die who had wasted his time on Earth. He didn't forgive his children, friends, etc. He died with unresolved issues and hardness in his heart. He died with unfulfilled dreams, hopes, and desires. He did not allow God to finish his story in its fullness.

If he had given God the pen to his life story, it would have ended differently.

We consider great generals like Oral Roberts, etc. who told God when they were ready to leave the Earth. This is the way God means for us to die. He means it to be on our terms. He wants us to live a long healthy fruitful life.

I also know of some people who said that God took their loved one early because He knew that person couldn't make it in the future. I don't know about that; however, I know that God wants each tree to fulfill its destiny. The tree must deny self. It must realize it's not about itself anymore and swallow its pride.

Pride causes us to harbor unforgiveness. It causes us to keep hindrances held between brothers in Christ. I know for me personally I have other spiritual leaders that the Lord required me to ask them to forgive me and they refused! They are still in ministry today! This is why we must be careful because we can be operating in signs miracles and wonders and go to hell! We may think we're right with God, but if we don't forgive someone else, we will not be forgiven! It's dangerous territory!

Forgive your brother. Forgive your family. Redeem the time, and ask God to help you make the most of your life. Leave a legacy. Don't leave this Earth without discovering how great the plans of God were for your life. Change the world. Be all that God has called you to be. Don't hold back. You cannot be successful without taking risks. If God tells you to do something, do it. Don't hesitate or reason it out in the flesh. There is a reason He asks you to do those things. He knows what He is doing. Trust in Him!

11

THE HIDDEN GARDEN OF
PRAYER & INTERCESSION

Our Secret Weapon

As His Bride, we have the honor and opportunity to talk to our Master any time of day. Not only can we talk to Him anytime we want, but we can talk to Him even while we are talking to someone else or doing something else. I hear some of you asking, "How can you do that?"

Well, this is a secret weapon that God has granted to His people. We have the Holy Spirit on the inside of us. Our spirit man is built for relationship with its Creator. The Bible says that we war against our flesh and our spirit.

This is what that means. Our spirit is from God, and it always wants a right relationship with God. However, our flesh is the attachments we've gathered while living in this world, and they war against goodness and righteousness. All of the demonic influences we've had hinder the fullness of our experience with God. However, the Holy Spirit comes in and helps us to win that battle. Let me explain:

We are a fresh plant coming into the atmosphere. We are straight from Heaven so we are beautiful, bright, and fluffy. We are happy to be here and enjoying the beautiful sunshine.

However, our big tree parents open the doors in the garden for the enemy to come and place nasty things on our pretty little plants. They allow violent spirits to come in through television shows, music, and the hardness of the atmosphere hurts our little plants. Our parent trees may fight all the time and their harsh words enter our plants and cause them to wither up. They may smack our plants around and be really mean to them; and the plants can barely breathe from all the harassments in the environment.

The plants may grow up playing video games, watching plants kill other plants, or blowing other plants up. The games may include trees being cut up and used for sacrifices of children, etc. So, as tender little plants, we're exposed to all this knowledge of the world and it attaches itself to our plants. We grow up with it still underneath our bark. We may grow tall and cover our wounds well, but they are still there.

Then, when we discover our true reason for existence and surrender to the Ultimate Gardener, we are again happy as we were before all of our attachments.

Following salvation, I learn how God wants to live on the inside of me to the fullness and be my guide. He wants to use my tree and change the whole forest! He wants to use little 'ole me to change the world! He wants to give me my own prayer language so that when I talk to Him, no other tree can know what I'm saying, and it's always the perfect will of my Creator.

He also wants to build a whole kingdom on the inside of my tree. So, now I have a Superpower on the inside of me, and no one can take that from me. I am a special tree! Now that I'm trying to obey that super-power with all of my might, the attachments keep trying to pull me back. The Superpower wants me to pray, but the attachments want me to play a video game. They want me to be like the other trees in the forest.

The attachments make fun of me now because I am different than the other trees. If I had the attachments of drugs, that attachment is still there saying, "Come on tree…you're sad, why don't you go get you some drugs to make you feel better." Those attachments are always warring against the will of God because we opened that door for the attachment to come in. This is why we need deliverance to rid ourselves of those attachments. I know some people do not believe you can have a demon after you get saved; however, it is so!

According to John Eckhardt's article on CharismaMag.com, "The ministry of deliverance is the covenant right of believers. Like every other blessing from God--healing, prosperity, miracles and so on--it is promised only to His covenant people, those who believe in Jesus and come to God through Christ's blood. God, in His mercy, will bless people outside the covenant because He is merciful. But primarily, His blessings are based on covenant." (Eckhardt, 2015)

The Weapon of the Garden

Now that we have established the war that rages inside due to our past versus the future that God desires, let me explain how we can have a conversation with our Superpower and not be moving our lips.

When your spirit man has connected with the Creator and asked Him to fill your tree with the Holy Ghost and power, the Superpower enters the tree and begins talking to it and leading it. As you build a relationship with Him through reading the Bible, prayer, and supplication, you begin to hear His voice and understand His ways. When you understand that still small voice of peace, then He can talk to you anytime, and you will hear Him. You have a choice whether to obey Him or continue living in sin.

However, He continues to convict and woo you. While He's giving you instructions, you can have a whole conversation with Him in your heart. Here is a scenario:

Holy Spirit - "Now June, you know that wasn't right that you said that. Repent to that person and make it right with them."

June – "But Lord, I had a right to say that. They were wrong, and I'm tired of them treating me that way. Don't you understand what they're doing to me? Go get 'em God!"

Holy Spirit – "I'm telling you to repent. You need to forgive that person as well."

June – (At this point, June has a choice on whether to act on this instruction or to harbor the bitterness. Also, as June is considering the answer the devil steps in on the conversation.)

Devil – "Now June, if you repent to Suzie Q, she will hate you the rest of her life, and there's no need to make matters worse. You were right in what you did, and there is no need for you to repent!"

June – (At this point, June must choose which road she will take.)

June – "OK God, please help me forgive that person because that really hurt. I choose to forgive Suzie Q, and I will call her right now."

June to Suzie Q – "Hello Suzie, the Lord convicted me over my behavior when I got mad at you, and I must repent. Please forgive me. I'm sorry for what I said, and I repent." (June waits on a reply from Suzie Q.)

Suzie Q - (At this point, Suzie Q has a choice to make on her end; however, June will not be held accountable for what Suzie Q does with the apology. June is only held accountable for obeying God and repenting and seeking Suzie Q's forgiveness.)

Suzie Q – "Thank you June. I forgive you, and please forgive me, too. (Now, healing flows between both parties.)

If Suzie Q would have chosen the bitterness route, her roots would be clogging up and be dangerous for her well-being).

June to God – "Thank you, God, for correcting me. Please help me forgive Suzie Q, and I release this situation to you, Lord. Please forgive me for hurting You in how I represented You to Suzie Q."

This example shows how all this has happened within two minutes, and most all of it was within me. I might be sitting in a restaurant chatting with friends, and this conversation is going on in my heart. We have this honor to have the garden within us so that we can have continual communication with our Creator at any time.

This is going to be vital in the days to come and persecution arising. We may have people approach us with guns to our heads asking us to renounce Christ or forfeit our lives. We can immediately enter our garden and talk to our Savior and Creator of all the Earth.

We can be sitting at a table in beautiful fellowship while all this chaos is going on around the Earth. We are not moved by the outer environment because the garden on the inside of us is solid. We are like big redwood trees in the forest.

We are 300 feet tall!! No matter what storms may come, we stand tall because our roots are solid in the garden!

One other thing I want to point out about the garden: This is an insert from my journal in 2013 about my discovery of the garden. This is from a post I put on Facebook.

October 10, 2013

Anyone who knows me and has been paying attention to my life this year knows that I've been in the trial of my life! God shut all the doors this year because he wanted me on my face seeking Him.

He let me know I've been "wandering" too long. We have business to do...children who need prayer...and a mother who needs to get back to her ministry. So, I went through five months of repentance, life-reflection, learning about God all over again, and experiencing Christ as His bride.

It's been the hardest trial of my life because my actions were so damaging previously. I was in and out of church so many times in my pain, and it caused so many ripple effects. So, he pressed me, and I wept constantly. I had people/friends tell me I was crazy for repenting so much. They said, "God would not be doing that. You're too hard on yourself." I kept telling them that God was causing me to "face myself" and it was not pretty to look at! Also, having so many people put me down and press me, I was constantly in the prayer closet crying.

I found the Lord like I've never known him. Now that I can see the top of the mountain, I reflect back on the days sitting on the big rock with the creek water running over my feet and me looking up to the sky and just loving on God. I look up to him and say, "You're such a great big God!" This is why I love praying outdoors. It's God all around me!

One time I spent all day at the creek, and I became thirsty. I said, "God, please bring me some water." About 30 minutes later a car showed up. They asked me what I was doing sitting in the creek. As I explained, I ended up sharing my testimony and the two women in the car sat there crying. I prayed for them and then they handed me a bottle of water!

I will miss those days at that creek! I almost want to make a memorial there because it was my "secret place" for five months and was where I built a solid relationship with God again. One day, I saw some random flowers growing. I picked them and took them to my friend who was very sad.

I told her that these were anointed flowers because it's where I fertilize the atmosphere with tears and prayers.

Communication with our Creator

God desires for His creation to spend time with Him in the Garden. Remember, this is why He created us to begin with. He wants us to go to that secret place in prayer and go into His chambers and talk with Him. He wants to restore our trees, refresh our trees, and wash our trees in His presence. It's a secret garden that no one can take from us. This is a special place between us and God. This is where we reveal our deepest secrets, deepest pains, our fears, joys, thanks, sorrows, etc. This is the place where we talk with our Daddy God. We can go into that closet, and sit upon His lap. We can talk to him just like we do our earthly dads.

Some people say one is selfish if he prays for himself. I beg to differ. How can we examine ourselves before our holy Creator if we can't be transparent with Him, and discuss the reasons we did things, and ask for His guidance? He wants to be our best friend, the one we lean upon, and the one we cry to, etc. He wants to be our everything.

This is why I chose the beautiful picture on the cover of this book. It displays a beautiful pure bride swinging in a garden. This is us when we are in communication and fellowship with such a magnificent Father! We can swing in rest in that garden! It's the place for us to get up in His lap and cry on His shoulders. He wants us to release that pain, etc., to Him! Who else do we talk to? Man? He can only help so far…but God created us so He has all the answers.

If you are reading this book and religion has crept in and taught you differently about prayer, I beg you to find a private place outside and look up into the heavens and just talk to Him.

161

He will hear you if you're sincere with a pure heart. My favorite way to pray is to go out into the woods alone with God. I like to sit on a rock with my feet waving in the creek, look up between the trees, and talk to my Creator. I like thinking how big He is and how great He is!

Being outside keeps me focused on knowing how He created everything! Suddenly my problems seem so small. I also like to worship Him outside. This is so liberating! Just dance out in the wide-open fields, singing to Him. Knowing that He's watching me and smiling is the best feeling! He saved us! He created us! He loves us! He knows us! He will never leave us or forsake us! He forgave us! He is awesome and worthy of all praise!

I'm going to tell a story that may shock you. It sounds so crazy but it did happen! When I travel, I love riding in my 2000 Toyota Camry with 250,000 miles on it, check engine light on and bald tires. LOL. (God recently blessed me with new tires).

Eyes of God Stopped to Watch Me

Anyways, I have a sunroof and I will pull that back, roll the windows down, and it becomes my traveling "secret place." I'm in the wide-open and I go to town! I will sing to Him, wave my hands in worship, look up to the sky and just smile at Him! I talk to Him and compliment His creation as I travel down the road, whether it's beautiful trees, sunset, hills, etc. So, one night last year while I was on the Summer Tour, I was deep into worship and it was at night. It was a warm summer night so I was living it up! I felt the moon shining on my head so I looked up through the car and saw all the beautiful stars by the beautiful moon that seemed to be right on me. I said, "Lord, I feel you smiling at me!" I was blushing! I could just feel the rays of His love and admiration over me!

162

Then all of a sudden I felt these eyes roll around the car (this is in the spirit), and they were hanging in front of the car just staring at me! I HAD GOD'S FULL ATTENTION!

I said, "Oh my Lord, are you staring at me? Not only are you smiling, but now you've stopped time to stare at me?" I was blushing from ear to ear! LOL. He stayed there for about 30 minutes with His presence all over me in that car! He was all around me! I felt like my body just lifted and went to the third heavens! It was a surreal moment. All I could say was, "Holy, Holy, Holy are you Lord!" I can't help but weep in His presence! Then He left me and I felt Him leave me. It was amazing! After this I found out that He has eyes that roam the Earth. Look at this:

> **2 Chronicles 16:9 For the eyes of the Lord run to and fro throughout the whole earth, to show Himself strong on behalf of those whose heart is loyal to Him.**

I encourage you to go outside and get real with God. Lay it all out there. He knows it anyway, but He wants to hear it from you! Think about how He did Adam and Eve. He knew they ate of the wrong tree, but He still asked them, didn't He? Yes, he did because He wanted them to be accountable for their actions. He expects the same from us. Remember I said earlier that David was after God's own heart, because He would confess His sin to God and be truthful even though he had sinned and offended God.

I hear some of you saying that you can't go outside because you're either in the nursing home, hospital or prison reading this. I encourage you to just talk to the Lord right where you're at. He can help you to find your garden. He wants to build a solid relationship with you and age has nothing to do with the garden!

Age, race, denomination, creed, nationality, etc., has nothing to do with your relationship with God in the garden! Your "secret place" may be different than other people, but He will still meet you there! I've preached to many prisoners and elderly in nursing homes. I tell them that God will meet them where they are at and they can leave a legacy with the time they have left!

God is just like an earthly daddy, but better. As long as you're honest about what you did, your dad will deal with it accordingly. God is the same way. However, the Heavenly Daddy wants to make you better, so He may show you something in your heart that you need to repent about so that you can be healed and not sin again. God desires us to be healed and not sin continually. He wants 100% obedience. He wants you free and walking in purity and holiness.

Although God wants you to be without spot or wrinkle, He knows that no human is perfect. We all fall short of the glory. However, He means in heart and spirit. He wants us pure of heart. When you are pure of heart and He rebukes you and chastises you about a sin, He wants you to repent and ask for His help to overcome that area. He knows you can't do things on your own. He merely wants you to humble yourself, and ask Him to take it from you. You must choose to not want that sin in your heart. Once you ask for His help, when that temptation comes again to you, you will be able to resist it. We ask God to help us to resist. We ask Him to give us strength to say, "No."

Praying in the Spirit through Tongues

The best way to pray is in tongues. You receive tongues through being filled with the Holy Ghost. Let me clarify that there are two different types of tongues. One is for the edification of the church.

The other is for your prayer language and it is a gift for everyone! How do you receive this gift? You can either have the elders of the church lay their hands on you or impart it, or you can just simply lift your hands and ask God to fill you with His Holy Spirit. I have spoken in tongues since I was 20 years old, so over 27 years now. My son received the baptism in the Holy Ghost at age five years old and spoke in tongues for two days!

I can answer a few things about this miraculous prayer language:

- It is meant for everyone. It is a gift to impart into us a prayer language so that we can communicate with God one-on-one to where no one or the devil can understand what we are saying.

- This language He gives us is unique like our DNA. We talk in another language, and we surrender our tongue to the Holy Spirit so that He can communicate with God. I told you that God is a trinity, which means three-in-one. He is Father God, Jesus the Son, and The Holy Spirit as the guide. We are created in His image.

- We see humans as one image, but they are made up of body, soul, and spirit. The soul is the mind, will, and emotions. This is the same way with Jesus. He is the image of God. We see Him but He is made up of Jesus the Son, God the Father, and the Holy Spirit. He told us before He ascended to the Father that He must go so that we could receive the Holy Spirit on Earth.

- We can pray in the spirit, and it is a perfect prayer to God. It is the Holy Spirit releasing seeds into the atmosphere from Heaven as we pray. Remember the audible seeds we release? This is another way to release them. However, when we release them this way, it is God's perfect will.

165

- It is much better to pray in tongues than to pray in your natural language. This is due to the fact that tongues are the perfect will of God.

- We can pray in tongues anytime, and no one else can understand it. For instance, if we were taken captive by terrorists, we could pray in tongues, and they couldn't understand us. It is a gift and a private language between us and God.

- The Bible says it strengthens our inner man when we pray in the spirit. It edifies us.

- I must differentiate between the prayer language tongues and the edification of it in churches. There is a difference between the two. Some say you can't speak in tongues unless you have an interpreter. That is true in the case of the gift of tongues and interpretation. However, it is a separate gift than being filled with the Holy Ghost.

- Tongues can save your life in the case of an emergency. In my second book, *Testimony of a Broken Bride*, I share a story about attending a church service where the pastor stops his sermon midstream and says, "I don't know who this is for, but if you don't leave your husband, he could kill you." I knew that was me. I was living in that for five years and had been praying for help. On the way home that night with my three kids in the car, I began praying in tongues and entering warfare. When I got home, I learned he had planned to kill us that night. The Holy Spirit warned me and protected me! Read my whole life story at www.gotreehouse.org.

- Tongues will take you into the presence of the Lord quickly. Oftentimes when I am worshipping the Lord, I will pray or sing in tongues.

- When I feel His presence covering me like a glove, I may be frozen in awe and wonder, or I may burst out into spontaneous dance and worship. I love being in a church where I can obey the Lord and worship Him with all that is within me. I love not having limits on how I express my love to Him. He is my everything.

- Sometimes when I pray in tongues, the Holy Spirit will take me into the throne room. What I mean by that is that He takes me to another realm. I enter into the presence of the Lord and have a God-encounter. Sometimes, He talks to me there or gives me open visions. In *Testimony of a Broken Bride*, I talk about when I was on the platform in Bible College in worship, and the Holy Spirit took me into the throne room. Once there, I had an encounter that changed the course of my destiny forever! This encounter was so powerful that He shook Rod Parsley and made him stop working and preach to the Bible College chapel service about WE ARE THE BRIDE. He confirmed what God revealed to me in the throne room! I cried the whole time.

Worship as Intercession

I must include the point that worship to God is warfare. It is intercession. Worship tears down the walls of the natural and releases your whole being to your Creator. When you worship God with your whole heart and dance before Him, it is so liberating.

It's like your bones, flesh, cells, and your whole being are reacting to the One you love. It's a romance beyond words. It's a surrender of the natural law to the spiritual law of love.

I think of David, the way he worshipped God almost naked and unabashedly in front of anyone.

He released his being to the creator and danced before Him to show Him how much he loves Him. God just loves it!

I encourage you that if you are not in a church that allows you to worship God freely with all your heart but you know God has called you do so, go into a field somewhere and let it out. You'll discover that it is where you truly desire to be.

Because our battle is not with flesh and blood, but is with the principalities and powers of the air, warfare through worship tears down walls and cast demons to flight. It breaks through sound barriers in the spirit and speaks volumes to the enemy and to God. It is an amazing warfare tool!

Here are a few scriptures to help your research: 2 Kings 18:13-19:37; Acts 21:1-17; Psalm 149:1-9; Proverbs 18:8; 1 Chronicles 15:29; Psalm 30:11.

Jesus in Intercession

Jesus provided the best example about intercession when He interceded before His crucifixion. The area He was in is called Gethsemane, which means grove of olive trees.

Revivalist Timothy Lovett from Alabama gave me a great analogy about Jesus and the olive tree.

According to Revivalist Tim Lovett, "When Jesus sweated drops of blood; it fertilized the very roots of the olive tree. Nowhere in the world are they as deep-rooted. The Olive Garden was where the wine press was and the place where Jesus was in agony. This is the place of surrender."

This is profound! So, I had to research the olive tree.

The Garden of Gethsemane (Luke 22:39-46)

Matthew 26:36-46

36 Then cometh Jesus with them unto a place called Gethsemane, and saith unto the disciples, Sit ye here, while I go and pray yonder.

37 And he took with him Peter and the two sons of Zebedee, and began to be sorrowful and very heavy.

38 Then saith he unto them, My soul is exceeding sorrowful, even unto death: tarry ye here, and watch with me.

39 And he went a little farther, and fell on his face, and prayed, saying, O my Father, if it be possible, let this cup pass from me: nevertheless not as I will, but as thou wilt.

40 And he cometh unto the disciples, and findeth them asleep, and saith unto Peter, What, could ye not watch with me one hour?

41 Watch and pray, that ye enter not into temptation: the spirit indeed is willing, but the flesh is weak.

42 He went away again the second time, and prayed, saying, O my Father, if this cup may not pass away from me, except I drink it, thy will be done.

43 And he came and found them asleep again: for their eyes were heavy.

44 And he left them, and went away again, and prayed the third time, saying the same words.

45 Then cometh he to his disciples, and saith unto them, Sleep on now, and take your rest: behold, the hour is at hand, and the Son of man is betrayed into the hands of sinners.

46 Rise, let us be going: behold, he is at hand that doth betray me.

Luke 22:39-46

39 And he came out, and went, as he was wont, to the Mount of Olives; and his disciples also followed him.

40 And when he was at the place, he said unto them, Pray that ye enter not into temptation.

41 And he was withdrawn from them about a stone's cast, and kneeled down, and prayed,

42 Saying, Father, if thou be willing, remove this cup from me: nevertheless not my will, but thine, be done.

43 And there appeared an angel unto him from heaven, strengthening him.

170

44 And being in an agony he prayed more earnestly: and his sweat was as it were great drops of blood falling down to the ground.

45 And when he rose up from prayer, and was come to his disciples, he found them sleeping for sorrow,

46 And said unto them, Why sleep ye? rise and pray, lest ye enter into temptation.

Mark 14:32-42

32 And they came to a place which was named Gethsemane: and he saith to his disciples, Sit ye here, while I shall pray.

33 And he taketh with him Peter and James and John, and began to be sore amazed, and to be very heavy;

34 And saith unto them, My soul is exceeding sorrowful unto death: tarry ye here, and watch.

35 And he went forward a little, and fell on the ground, and prayed that, if it were possible, the hour might pass from him.

36 And he said, Abba, Father, all things are possible unto thee; take away this cup from me: nevertheless not what I will, but what thou wilt.

37 And he cometh, and findeth them sleeping, and saith unto Peter, Simon, sleepest thou? couldest not thou watch one hour?

38 Watch ye and pray, lest ye enter into temptation. The spirit truly is ready, but the flesh is weak.

39 And again he went away, and prayed, and spake the same words.

40 And when he returned, he found them asleep again, (for their eyes were heavy,) neither wist they what to answer him.

41 And he cometh the third time, and saith unto them, Sleep on now, and take your rest: it is enough, the hour is come; behold, the Son of man is betrayed into the hands of sinners.

42 Rise up, let us go; lo, he that betrayeth me is at hand.

Forgiveness in the Garden
Prophet Mark D. White
At God's Place in Clarksville, TN
October 20, 2013

It's like Jesus approached Judas in the garden. He gave Judas a chance of restoration and said, "Friend, why comest thou?" See Judas gave Jesus the kiss of betrayal.

Jesus gave Judas the words and opportunity of repentance, and Jesus could not have gone to the cross as the perfect sacrifice without maintaining the attitude in his life as he cried out, "My God, My God, why have you forsaken me?" (White, 2013)

It's in the garden where we can find forgiveness. It's in the garden where we can find the strength to love our enemies. It's in the garden where we find peace in the midst of the turmoil in our lives.

Birthing in the Spirit

Serious intercessors can birth a vision, dream, etc., into the world in the spirit. They are birthing a seed from Heaven into the atmosphere. I've experienced this before:

Birthing in We are the Bride Ministries

This was May 2015. I was headed to Florida for a women's conference. Halfway there I stayed the night with my son who lives in Alabama. The next day, as soon as I got on the interstate, I started smelling the most beautiful aroma. I was soaking it in like very deep breaths. All of a sudden, the PRESENCE OF GOD FILLED MY CAR! He covered me like a glove!

I can't even explain the experience except I just starting praying and weeping in the spirit. THEN, I STARTED BIRTHING AS I'M DRIVING DOWN THE INTERSTATE!!! YES! I had never done that before! It was so supernatural. He was DOWNLOADING revelation as I was driving, and WAVES OF HIS GLORY kept filling my car!

Wave after wave after wave of His presence kept flooding me and my car. It was like being in ecstasy in His presence! This lasted three hours! I birthed all the way to Florida.

So holy! I was groaning, travailing, weeping, and basically warring in another realm. Spiritual birthing is warfare! It is allowing the Holy Ghost to use you to break through barriers in the spirit.

I experienced this one other time as I'm finishing these books. I'm in my cabin and I'm finishing my last book:

Birthing in the Garden Books

It was a beautiful sunny Monday morning and I'm deeply concentrating on the book as I'm typing. All of a sudden the Holy Spirit comes in the room and about knocks me over on the bed. His power comes on me so strong I could hardly breathe. The glory was so strong! I started weeping uncontrollably, groaning, etc. He did same thing as He did before. He downloaded revelation into me! It was so deep I could hardly contain it in my earthly vessel. This happened every two hours! He would come on me so strong and I'd lie on the bed groaning and weeping.

That night I was at my host lady's house eating, Mrs. Joyce Guidry, and after we ate dinner she asked me, "What are your covers going to look like?" I started to answer her and all of a sudden here he came again! He about knocked me over at the table. I started weeping and said, "I need to go pray. Please forgive me." She knew what I was going through because she is a midwife. She is an intercessor and God divinely put me on her land to give birth to these books. She gave me a motor home that is on the back part of this property. She prays for me while I write. She's my intercessor and spiritual mother.

She made me curtains, fixed it up pretty, and painted me a sign that says, "Little Cabin on the Hill". She also soaked it in prayer and asked angels to be with me in this cabin.

Here's a picture:

Please see Pepper the sheepdog sitting there and my glory car.

Going back to the topic of birthing; I found an article online which best describes this experience:

"Travail and Apostolic Order"
By Bishop W. Peter Morgan

So now, let's define the word "TRAVAIL" which is pivotal, central and momentous to the Church which is you and me.

"The noun travail has two senses [1] concluding state of pregnancy; from the onset of labor to the birth of a child. [2] use of physical or mental energy; hard work.

And the verb travail has [1] sense which is to "work" hard. The word travail is used rarely in both the noun and verb form. Synonyms of the noun form of travail are: parturiency; lying-in; confinement; childbed; labor; for example: she was in labor for six hours.

Or Meronyms [parts of travail]: uterine contraction [a rhythmic tightening in labor of the upper uterine musculature that contracts the size of the uterus and pushes the fetus toward the birth canal]; effacement [shortening of the uterine cervix and thinning of its walls as it is dilated during labor].

"SO WHAT DOES TRAVAILING IN THE SPIRIT MEAN SINCE THIS IS EXACTLY WHAT WE AS THE CHURCH HAS TO DO AND DO SO ALWAYS?

"Paul, the Apostle did travail on behalf of others in the Spirit until the Spirit of Christ was formed in those in whom God has placed on his heart. Travailing in the Spirit means to travail or labor as in giving birth just as a woman in the natural travails when she is about to deliver her child. Spiritual travail is a level of intensity marked by a Holy Spirit burden to actually bring to pass, through prayer, a given promise, a prophetic insight or a Holy Spirit illuminated need in a person, church, city or nation." (Morgan, 2010)

This article best describes birthing. It is an amazing spiritual experience. As I'm finishing this book, the revelation he's downloading is so deep, and I beg Him to allow me to properly articulate this to my readers! I pray He's imparting revelation to you as you're reading this!

12

AN APPEAL TO HEAVEN

The Appeal to Heaven flag is significant to American history. We were calling on the country to pray and appeal to Heaven for our nation! Today, God is calling each Christian to appeal to Heaven on behalf of his own tree! God wants to bring revival to the human spirit, one tree at a time. As we repent, God will heal our nation! It begins with us!

The above picture is Pastor David Meeks and Pastor Marvin Adkins at World Outreach Revival Center on February 24, 2016

Surrender your tree to Him today, and allow your spirit to make an appeal to Heaven and bring revival to your heart.

Revival in Your Tree

As we return our trees to the Ultimate Creator and surrender the destiny book back to Him, revival will be born. How do we grow our trees and make them strong? By the word of God. The Bible is the source of food for survival.

We plant our roots deep in the Word of God, and let the glory of Jesus be the sunshine to our tree for nourishment! He will revive our trees!

Isaiah 37:31 – And the remnant that is escaped of the house of Judah shall again take root downward, and bear fruit upward.

We must drop all ideologies, the way we've been taught, our predisposed opinions about Christianity, our denominations, our traditions, our dogmas, and all preconceived beliefs about God and our relationship to Him. We must get alone with Him in the prayer closet, throw our hands up to Heaven, and say, "God, reveal yourself to me. Show me the truth. Teach me to rely solely on You and not on man-made doctrines or opinions. I want to discover You for myself.

Are We Reflecting His Beauty?

When you learn that the Holy Spirit is real and wants to be your best friend to teach you about God and your mission, some revelations will blow your mind. It is so different than the way you've been taught. It is so different than even the way the present-day Church is doing things. It will bring you to a point where you say, "God help me. I don't even know how to address this issue or what to do with the information you're giving me. How do I handle this?" You will be shocked to discover the truth. Once you do, you will be free in your spirit because God, Himself revealed it to you. Let others be liars. God's Word is truth!

I understand that some things can be read out of context, thus you must have spiritual moms and dads to whom you can go with questions. However, if their answers do not bear witness with the Holy Ghost within you, don't receive it. Trust God 100%. When God tells you to do something, always obey, and remember not everyone will like what He says. Trust in God, and know you are hearing His voice.

Once you make your appeal to Heaven and God reveals Himself and shocks you with the revelation, then you're on the road to revival because you have been awakened to His presence, His glory, the truth, and His love. Revival is being revived. You will be revived to natural order of things between you and your Creator. You are back in the garden having fellowship and relationship with the One you love. You are walking in 100% obedience to your Father, and you know that no matter what trial you are experiencing, He will be with you through it all and that it's for a reason.

Another reason we need to make an appeal to Heaven is on behalf of our nation. This is specifically for the American Bride. We must make an appeal to God on behalf of the decisions that our country has made in opposition to His will for this land.

We have taken abominable acts and paraded them all over the White House, which is the chief house in the land. We have made a mockery of God's name to the world, and we will answer to God for it. We must appeal to Heaven for mercy to fall on our nation and for revival in the people's hearts so that they may repent.

Only repentance will save our nation. God help the United States of America! If you're reading this from another country, please pray for us as well. The US Christians are very aware of the condition of our country.

> *Proverbs 12:12 – The wicked desireth the net of evil men: but the root of the righteous yieldeth fruit.*

Our appeal to Heaven is in prayer and crying out to a Holy God who is righteous, pure, and full of justice. He has a destiny for lands as well. The United States made a covenant with God, and we will answer for backing out of that covenant. We have a destiny to fulfill. We must pray for that destiny to be fulfilled.

Strengthening Our Roots for Revival

Root systems of trees are amazing. Remember the dream I had about the arrows hitting the tree and a spirit coming out of the arrows and clogging up the roots? It's because when we are reconnected to our Creator, the roots are flowing in the rivers of living water. Those rivers keep us refreshed to where we can bear much fruit. Look at what the Bible says about roots:

Like I said earlier, we are either going to burn on fire for God on Earth and allow Him to judge us while we're alive, or we are going to burn on fire in Hell in judgement following.

We must bear fruit for Him on Earth.

> *Matthew 3:10 – And now the axe is laid unto the root of the trees: therefore every tree which bringeth not forth good fruit is hewn down, and cast into the fire.*

How beautiful this river must be! Isn't it amazing that the Tree of LIFE is by a river? It's symbolism of what we experience in the spirit when we are right before God.

> *John 7:37-38*
>
> *37 - In the last day, that great day of the feast, Jesus stood and cried, saying, If any man thirst, let him come unto me, and drink.*
>
> *38 He that believeth on me, as the scripture hath said, out of his belly shall flow rivers of living water.*

The rivers of living water are Heaven flowing through us via the word of God, prayer, and especially praying in tongues. Praying in the spirit keeps our spirit man alive and keeps our flesh under control. We are able to walk in the spirit and allow the rivers to flow out of us. Another way to see the rivers flowing out is through our fresh fruit.

> *Matthew 12:33 - Either make the tree good, and his fruit good; or else make the tree corrupt, and his fruit corrupt: for the tree is known by his fruit.*

If a tree is rotten, it will bring forth rotten fruit. If a tree is righteous, it brings forth righteous fruit. We want our trees to bear much fruit for Him and especially fruit that remains!

Our hope in God makes us pure. We build up our most holy faith by communicating with God and spending time with Him. We allow Him to prune our trees.

We allow Him to remove viruses that have attached itself to us and to remove insects that try to feed off of us. We are a tree in His great garden, and we want to be a light to other trees around us. We want to shine with the glory of God on our trees and produce fruit that will remain.

Matthew 7:17-20

17 Even so every good tree bringeth forth good fruit; but a corrupt tree bringeth forth evil fruit.

18 A good tree cannot bring forth evil fruit, neither can a corrupt tree bring forth good fruit.

19 Every tree that bringeth not forth good fruit is hewn down, and cast into the fire.

20 Wherefore by their fruits ye shall know them.

The Bible says we can judge one another by the fruits we bear. God judges us by our hearts because on the outside, our trees can be dressed very well. We can put on a good show for the forest and make them think we're healthy, good trees, but God judges underneath all that bark. He knows the root system that tree is operating under. I took a picture one day of some bad roots on a tree.

This trees roots are all exposed. If a storm came it would blow this tree over. It doesn't look very secure.

Look at these pretty trees.

This tree is in Louisiana. Isn't it beautiful? It is by a beautiful pond.

These trees are in Mississippi. Beautiful!

This is a tree in Detroit. I felt sorry for it because it was all alone with no LIFE on it and behind bars. It's like some prisoners I visit.

These trees are in Ashland City, Tennessee. Look how beautiful as the colors change in the fall. They are beside a body of water and just reflecting on the water to the glory of God.

I imagine this tree standing so tall and beautiful to God just clapping its hands and praising its Creator.

I imagine this tree just basking in the glory of God. The sun shining on it brings the radiance of Heaven. I imagine the tree in photosynthesis and the cells soaking in the beautiful sunshine. I imagine the tree smiling to the Creator and saying, "Thank you for the sunshine and relief."

We should all be appreciative like this tree.

Revival in our trees knows who we are in Christ and our role on this Earth, that we only have one LIFE to live and a very short amount of time to leave a legacy. How sad it would be to live here and leave no footprints of our lives!

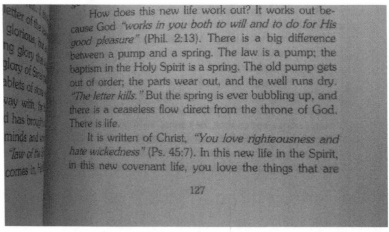

How does this new life work out? It works out because God *"works in you both to will and to do for His good pleasure"* (Phil. 2:13). There is a big difference between a pump and a spring. The law is a pump; the baptism in the Holy Spirit is a spring. The old pump gets out of order; the parts wear out, and the well runs dry. *"The letter kills."* But the spring is ever bubbling up, and there is a ceaseless flow direct from the throne of God. There is life.

It is written of Christ, *"You love righteousness and hate wickedness"* (Ps. 45:7). In this new life in the Spirit, in this new covenant life, you love the things that are

127

I had to include this in my book from Smith Wigglesworth! Powerful! (Wigglesworth, 2001)

lavishly offers! You can never be ordinary from the day you receive this life from above. You become extraordinary, filled with the extraordinary power of our extraordinary God.

We do become extraordinary when we surrender 100% to God!

where God is pouring out His Spirit and yet miss the blessing that God is so willing to bestow. This is all due to a lack of revelation and a misunderstanding of the infinite grace of God and of *"the God of all grace"* (1 Pet. 5:10), who is willing to give to all who will reach out the hand of faith. This life that He freely bestows is a gift. Some think they have to earn it, and they miss the whole thing. Oh, for a simple faith to receive all that God so lavishly offers! You can never be ordinary from the day you receive this life from above. You become extraordinary, filled with the extraordinary power of our extraordinary God.

How sad would it be to live on this Earth and never learn the plan that God had for your tree? Don't put it off any longer! Dive into the waters of faith, Bride!

on the sick in His name (Mark 16:18).

The *"exceedingly great and precious promises"* (2 Pet. 1:4) of the Word are given to us that we might be *"partakers of the divine nature"* (v. 4). I feel the Holy Spirit is grieved with us when we know these things but do not do greater deeds for God. Does not the Holy Spirit show us wide-open doors of opportunity? Will we not let God lead us to greater things? Will we not believe God to take us on to greater demonstrations of His power? He calls us to forget the things that are behind, reach toward the things ahead, and *"press toward the goal for the prize of the upward call of God in Christ Jesus"* (Phil. 3:13–14).

105

If I kept looking in the rear-view mirror, I would not be writing this book. I would not be having HOPE for tomorrow, knowing that God can turn it all around. He will turn the bad into good! He's a good God!

good treasures. When we *"regard iniquity in [our hearts],
the Lord will not hear"* us (Ps. 66:18); and it is only as
we are made righteous, pure, and holy through the precious blood of God's Son that we can enter into this life
of holiness and righteousness in the Son. It is the righteousness of our Lord Himself made real in us as our faith
remains in Him.

After I was baptized with the Holy Spirit, the Lord
gave me a blessed revelation. I saw Adam and Eve
turned out of the Garden for their disobedience. They
were unable to partake of the Tree of Life, for the cheru-
bim with flaming sword kept them away from this tree.
When I was baptized, I saw that I had begun to eat of
this Tree of Life, and I saw that the flaming sword surrounded it. It was there to keep the devil away. Oh, what
privileges are ours when we are born of God! How mar-
velously He keeps us so that the wicked one cannot
touch us. I see a place in God where the enemy does not
dare to come. We are *"hidden with Christ in God"* (Col.
3:3). He invites us all to come and share this wonderful
hidden place. We dwell *"in the secret place of the Most
High"* and *"abide under the shadow of the Almighty"*
(Ps. 91:1). God has this place for you in this blessed
realm of grace.

Peter went on to say, *"As His divine power has
given to us all things that pertain to life and godliness
through the knowledge of Him who called us by glory
and virtue"* (2 Pet. 1:3). God is calling us to this realm of
glory and virtue. We, as we feed on His *"exceedingly
partakers of*

190

Smith Wigglesworth makes a very good point. We can get to a place where the devil cannot touch us. It must be a place of 100% obedience. It must be a place where our flesh is under subjection to the spirit. It must be a place where the old man no longer exists.

The revival that we are all praying about will be in every heart. It is not like the revivals of old where it was one person leading a revival. It will be in every heart. It will also be the nobody's that do not have a name. They are the ones that have been hid in caves and God is about to reveal.

13

ORGANIC CHRISTIANITY
BACK TO THE GARDEN

According to Apostle Pat Ehmann, "God is bringing us back to the original. He is bringing us back to what destroyed us, which is obedience. We lost the relationship in the garden due to disobedience. God is going to restore us. He wants us to be the true sons of God." (Ehmann, 2015)

On January 9, 2016, at The Hub Gathering in Hattiesburg, Mississippi, Prophetic Revivalist Ron Teal said, "In 2016, God is bringing back identity. It's bringing us back to who God originally created us to be." (The Hub Gathering, 2016)

Both of these are in agreement that God is wooing His Church back to its original intention. We are The Church! It's not a building. He is jealous over this tree, and He wants it all to Himself. He wants her to know who she is in Him so that she can fulfill the destiny that God has for her, which has been written in the Destiny Books before time began.

God wants His children pulled away from processed Christianity. This process is where man put his hand in it and stirred his beliefs and doctrines into the pot. The process is where man dictated to other people what God was saying.

It's a processed Christianity where we have built traditions, cultures, beliefs, and expectations of God. We have added ingredients that were not of the original design.

God wants His children to come back into the Garden and fellowship with Him. He wants the children to lay their hearts out there to Him and let Him clean them up and purify them. He wants to clean the plants and remove the attached viruses, bumps, bugs, mold, and other added ingredients that were not meant to be there. He wants to hold that tree in His hand and pull off the bad branches that were holding that tree back from growing tall and fluffy. He wants to prune the tree to make it go back to the design He meant it to be.

God wants to take that tree's roots and wash them in the rivers. He wants to dip them in the crystal clear waters that are from the rivers of living water. He wants to take the clogged up root that has been sitting in the waters not receiving from the rivers for 20 years, break it open, and pull the virus out. He wants to shake that root and command it to be healed so that the rivers can flow from that root. Once the rivers flow through that old rotten root, it will climb up the tree and come out the branches and bear fruit for Him. He knows you can't do this on your own. It is going to take the supernatural power of God to do this. All He needs is for you to surrender your tree back to Him.

Trees That Have Been in the Storms – The Beaten Trees

At this cabin (camper) where I've been writing these books, it is so peaceful. It's on a 120 acre farm with horses, chickens, and a big fluffy sheep-dog that is just a puppy and jumps on you all the time. They have such beautiful trees here. There are pine trees, oak trees, and many other trees. There is also a beautiful pond to look at every morning when I pray and at night when the sun sets.

We have a sign hanging on the front porch that says, "Little Cabin on the Hill." We posted that because God always puts me in a cabin when He wants me to write a book.

Last night, we had a tornado, and this trailer was being beaten really hard with the winds. I lay on the floor praying and thinking about these trees. They have weathered Hurricane Katrina (the biggest hurricane in US history) and the violent winds of last night. One tree that is next to my front porch is sideways because of Hurricane Katrina. It split the tree in half. I look at it and think of how brave that tree is. It has weathered many storms and still stands strong. This is how God wants us to be.

I had to insert this picture. It's a big oak tree on the back of the property. I pray underneath this tree. It is so peaceful out here.

When I was leaving the prayer spot, I took a picture of the trunk

of the tree and noticed it is two trees combined into one! It's a twin tree! How prophetic! This is the beautiful field it's in. The big oak tree is in the back of that field.

If we have our roots deeply planted in Him, He will carry us through every storm that comes our way. The key is to keep our roots in the rivers of living water. This is supernatural as I explained earlier in the Salvation experience. Once we accept Him, our roots supernaturally grow into the rivers. Our hearts are beautiful, pink, and fleshy-looking when we are in repentance and humble.

When we allow sin in, it hardens our hearts, clogs our roots, and the rivers begin to slow down their effect upon our tree. This will affect the fruit we grow and produce for God. God judges us on the fruit we produce for Him. He wants us to grow an abundance of fruit, and He is the One who is able to eat from our trees and be satisfied. He is able to say, "This tree is very pleasing to my heart. She gives her life away and obeys me."

Trust God in the storms. I prayed with a prisoner one day who asked me, "Please pray for me, I am so devastated because I lost custody of my children today. The judge took my parental rights." I saw that he was such a sad tree. My heart went out to him. Even though he's in prison, he is still a father and loves his children. I know the Holy Ghost gave me this answer. "Sir, we love Him when He says yes and we love Him when He says no.

He just cried on my shoulders. This is how we are with God. Although we do not understand what He is doing, we trust Him anyway. I have reached my hand into the storm and pulled myself out when I was suffering, and it cost me and my family greatly. I didn't wait for God to work it out in His own time.

It would be easy now for me to just walk away and quit because I've been in the pit and fire for almost three years. I've been homeless, living with other people, not able to get a job, obeying God amongst great persecution, etc. I've been through it. However, I learned my lesson not to reach into the storm and pull myself out.

It is very easy to do that! It's harder to keep your roots planted and holding your branches up to God and screaming, "I LOVE YOU ANYWAY! I TRUST YOU ANYWAY! I WILL NEVER LEAVE YOU AGAIN! YOU ARE GOD! YOU ARE HOLY! I TRUST YOU!" We praise Him anyway! We love Him anyway!

We have His Word that says He will work it out, and it will all pan out in the end. Those who wait upon the Lord shall renew their strength and shall mount up with wings as eagles!

> *Isaiah 40:31 - But they that wait upon the Lord shall renew their strength; they shall mount up with wings as eagles; they shall run, and not be weary; and they shall walk, and not faint.*

Trust Him Bride!

14

DR. JUNE DAWN KNIGHT'S TREE

In order to understand why God chose me to write this book about the twin books in this hour, you must understand my past and where God has brought me from. You can read the full story in the first book of this series, *Testimony of a Broken Bride; Jesus is the True Husband*. God took my mess, shame, and failures and made this woman pure and holy for Him! He's amazing! This is a summary of my LIFE:

My LIFE as of 02/15/16

CHILDHOOD FACTS

- Mother/Father divorced at 5 years-old.
- Both parents were alcoholics & abusive
- Sexually molested by family members
- Grandmother spirit-filled & imparted into June on death bed at about 7 years-old.
- Birthed a hunger inside June for God
- 10 years-old got saved through Billy Graham on television

10 YEARS TO 20 YEARS

- Went to a country Baptist Church by bus
- Prayed in woods and heard God talk to her
- Pastor of church kicked her out due to telling truth. Humiliated her in front of church
- Left church at 11 years-old
- At 12 years-old lost virginity to neighbor
- Met future husband at 14 years-old

10-20 CONT'D

- Mother kicked out of house at 15 yo.
- Married on 16th Birthday
- Had first child a month before 18th bday
- Dabbled in Occult – Ouija Board/Witchcraft at 19 years-20 years-old – Became Demon-Possessed.
- At 20 years-old – 1st Assembly church cast demons out and got filled with Holy Ghost.

21 – 25 YEARS OLD

- Started 1st AG and traveled to cast demons out, operating in prophetic.
- During 5 years of ministry, husband rejected God and became severely abusive.
- At end of marriage (9 yrs later), Lord spoke to June and said, "I want you all to myself because I'm a jealous God".
  - June's response – "Are you saying I can never be married again?"
  - God said it again – "I want you ALL TO MYSELF."
  - June responded – "No, I'm not that woman."

25 - 35 YEARS OLD

- **After divorce from 1st husband, married 5 more times in rebellion to God!**
  - Married kid's dad 2 more times
  - Married man and lasted 3 weeks
  - Married another man lasted 1 ½ years
  - Married another man lasted 1 day!

36 YEARS OLD - CONFRONTATION W/GOD

- God comes back at 36 and says it again – **"I said, I want you ALL TO MYSELF BECAUSE I'M A JEALOUS GOD."**
  - *June replies, "Lord, you're still asking me this 5 marriages later? I'm not this woman..please go find a virgin who hasn't had the life I've had! I'm severely; codependent. Please don't ask me to do this."*
  - *God replies, "June, If you will trust me, I will show you what a REAL husband is! I will take care of you!"*
  - *June answers call and says, "Yes Lord." June gets baptized and marries the Lord that day.*
    - *Four days later he wakes her up at 4 a.m. and tells her to go to World Harvest Bible College! Sell her house and give away everything she has and FOLLOW HIM!*
    - *Two months later she was in Columbus, Ohio.*

202

36 YEARS – 46 YEARS-OLD

- Went to WHBC at 36 years old
- God does miracles and shows her how He is ALL she needs!
- We are the Bride Ministries was born on the platform in Chapel in the throne room!
- God sent Rod Parsley to preach to me that day about WE ARE THE BRIDE!
- Lord told June she was going to write a book called WE ARE THE BRIDE and tell the world how He is the TRUE HUSBAND.
- June's reply to God, "Lord, I didn't even graduate high school. I have no education. How can I write a book?"
- Lord woke June up 8 months into Bible College and told her, "I have a present for you...I'm going to let you get married again!"
- June's response, "Why now after all I've done?
- God said, "You had to love ME before you could ever love a man!"

CONT'D

- Did not graduate from WHBC due to quitting during suffering
- Following WHBC, went to college:
  - Bachelor's Degree – Public Relations
  - Master's Degree – Corporate Communications
    - Studied in London under top three global marketing/advertising/media firms.
    - School paid for education.
    - They offered to send me to get doctorate and GOD SAID NO.
    - School stripped me of honors and persecuted me last semester.
- After graduation God stopped June and said, "Get on your face and get right with me."
  - Once in throne room, God said, "Serve my people with what you learned in school. I am your boss."
  - I lost it all due to obedience and been in PIT for three years since.

203

46 TO 47 YEARS-OLD

- International Miracle Institute called me and offered me a doctorate in theology and $10,000 off! God said YES!
- I graduated August 2015! God paid for it supernaturally too!
- Started We are the Bride Ministries in January 2015. Started WATB Radio and WATB.tv and have interviewed over 200 ministers from all over the world in one year.
- Started TreeHouse Publishers in January 2015 when published first book, *Selling the Mark of the Beast: Marketing RFID, EU vs. US*
- My whole three years has been totally by faith!
- I've prayed for people on their death bed for 1 ½ years
- Summer 2015 I went on a National Tour and met all kinds of ministries all over and told them about radio and WATB.tv. I've interviewed CHIEF APOSTLES in TX, LA, MS, IA, MI, and OH. I've also conducted Round Table shows as well!
- After the tour I wrote my 2nd book, *Testimony of a Broken Bride: Jesus Is the True Husband.* This is my life story.

CURRENT FACTS ABOUT DR. JUNE

- Coming out of PIT.
- All equipment on fritz
- Been single now 15 years.
- Living 100% by faith
- Feel that God is raising up a pure, unadulterated media to where it will not be tainted.
  - God has sifted me, purged me and cleansed me to prepare me for this. I became the woman I fought Him about.
  - This media has been focusing on the Christians in the caves. The hidden ones that have NOT had a voice. It PROVIDES them a voice.

WE ARE THE BRIDE MINISTRIES & TREEHOUSE PUBLISHERS

- **We are the Bride –** www.wearethebride.us.
- **WATB Radio –** www.watbradio.com
- **WATB.tv –** www.watb.tv
- **TreeHouse Publishers –** www.gotreehouse.org

BUILDING PROMISE & SMITH WIGGLESWORTH

- God told me two weeks before I left on trip to pray for building.
- Two days before I left, He told me to go lay hands ON BUILDING. He gave me vision of what it looked like.
- After research, I found it. It's the old WLAC building in Nashville.
- I took staff and went to lay hands on it. Went into open vision (will explain in next page).
- Found out through research that night that this radio station is very historical in US. Created a NEW SOUND. Birthed TV.
- That night God gave June dream and told her to go BACK that there was land for sale next to it and TO PROCLAIM IT ALL FOR THE BRIDE! DON'T ASK FOR SMALL WHEN IT COMES TO MY BRIDE! So, we all went back and poured anointed water and proclaimed it for the bride! It's three BIG LOTS on prime land near interstate!!!
- Three states later receive call from Dr. Judy Laird and God told her to give me the book, Smith Wigglesworth, and to bury it on the land as a prophetic gesture of the LAST GREAT AWAKENING!
- So, have had the Bride all over America sign this book since then in prophetic gesture that they are coming into agreement for new media!

OPEN VISION ON LAND!!! JUNE 2015

- I was walking beside radio station headed back to car and went into an open vision.
- I saw the biggest tent they make in the front lawn with cars parked up and down main highway.
- Cars parked all on the land! People coming from all over the world!
- I saw people packed inside the tent and outside in the lawn.
- I saw television cameras and radio inside tent BROADCASTING TO THE WORLD WHAT WAS GOING ON!
- I come out of the vision screaming, "OH MY GOD...YOU WANT THE LAST GREAT AWAKENING ON THIS LAND! YES LORD, YES LORD! WE CLAIM THIS FOR THE BRIDE! IT'S FOR YOUR BRIDE!"

DR. JUNE DAWN KNIGHT
SPIRITUAL FATHERS

Dr. Rod Parsley

Dr. Christian Harfouche

both have same spiritual father,

Dr. Lester Sumrall and Smith Wigglesworth

Prophet Ron Teal – Alabama

Pastor David Meeks - Mississippi

Pastor Marvin Adkins - Mississippi

Dr. Robin Harfouche –
Global Apostolic Faith Church, Pensacola, FL
Dr. Dianna Senkyrik –
Eagleheart Ministries – Bay City, TX
Apostle Pat Ehmann –
The Hub Gathering – Hattiesburg, MS
Intercessor Joyce Gidry –
World Outreach Revival Center, Picayune, MS
Intercessor Ruth Powers –
World Outreach Revival Center, Picayune, MS
Pastor Shirley Meeks –
World Outreach Revival Center, Picayune, MS

I included my life story because I wanted you to see how God is shifting my life story since I returned the pen to my life story to Him. I had no idea He had this planned for me. When I was in grad school, I merely wanted to work in a public relations firm and make big money. I thought I had big dreams. That heart's desire is nothing compared to what God had in store for me before time began. I'm very thankful I gave Him the pen and released my will to His. My story will end beautifully, and I will be able to enjoy eternity with the one I am so in love with!

Let Your Light So Shine Before Men

This is the day that I turn this book in for print and the Lord woke me up and told me to include the dream of the translucent butterfly. After He told me, I said, "This will be perfect because the whole book is about being pure and translucent before a Holy God." This book reflects my relationship with God and I pray it has blessed you and stirred your spirit for intimacy with Him.

Dream of My Translucent Butterfly

I was a butterfly hanging on a tree. I knew it was my time to fly so I let go of the tree and was flying through the beautiful field of flowers then crossed over the hill into a beautiful field of wheat. There was MILLIONS of wheat!

I stopped in the middle of that field and my butterfly GREW AS BIG AS THE WHEAT! I hovered over the millions...my wings spanned out as far as they reached...all the way around!

Then the sun shined from Heaven and shined right through the butterfly! The iridescent colors just glistened on the wheat! So many different colors and sparkles! It was so bright and beautiful! I could see the various colors rolling over the wheat as the light guided it. I saw pinks, purples, yellows, reds, blues, greens, etc. The colors shined on the wheat like rays of sunshine.

Then...the wheat starts clapping their hands! They were in awe of the rays of beauty from the sun! They all stood there clapping in amazement.

Then, suddenly, God's hand, as big as the sky, came down and swiped up the butterfly and took it to Heaven with him!

Notes about the dream:

I now realize that the tree was the Tree of Life. I've been feeding off of that tree gaining my strength to shine to the world. Remember the other dream God gave me about the Tree providing all the fruit for me? This is the same tree! God revealed this tree to me here in Picayune, Mississippi. This town is a very special place and is a refuge for the prophets. The Lord gave me a dream a couple of weeks ago and told me to write a book called Pic a June: Picayune, Mississippi – Refuge for the Prophets. Stay tuned...

15

PRAYER TO FIND THE GARDEN

I pray this book has caused you to re-examine your relationship with God. I pray that it set a fire within your soul to want to draw closer to Him in an intimate, passionate relationship. I pray that you see the beauty of His holiness all around you. I pray that you see the beautiful red birds that He created. I pray you see the beautiful mountains that look so majestic. I pray you see the beautiful trees that provide us with oxygen, food, and beauty. I pray that you see God in your surroundings. This Earth was created for us.

I pray this book has helped you to understand God as the Creator of all. I mean that you see Him as such a big God that nothing is impossible for Him. Your faith level will rise as you discover WHO He really is. I pray that you worship Him in a reckless abandonment to His glory. I pray that you drop traditions, expectations of religion, opinions of mankind, and all of your pre-conceived ideals and discover a very real God who is standing at the door and knocking to enter the secret places of your heart.

> *Revelation 3:20 – Behold I stand at the door and knock: If any man hear my voice, and open the door, I will come in to him and sup with him, and he with me.*

Dear God,

I surrender all. Please forgive me for any acts of disobedience I've done in my past. (Name them if you know them.) Reveal yourself and your Holy Spirit to me. Help me, God, to walk according to Your destiny book that You wrote for me before time began. I want to live the fullest LIFE that You have designed for me. I cancel any negative word that's been spoken against my destiny or my LIFE! I renounce any allegiance to Satan I've made in my LIFE. I renounce any acts that I've done willingly or unknowingly that made a pact with the enemy.

I refuse to live a mediocre LIFE. I want to follow You to the ends of the Earth in full obedience to Your will. Thank You for making my crooked paths straight.

I please the blood of Jesus over my eyes (eye gate), my ears (ear gate), my mouth (mouth gate), and over my heart. I pray you cover me with your wings and place me underneath that dome of protection.

I surrender my tree back to the perfect Ultimate Gardener. Please heal my roots of any bitterness from over the years.

I forgive everyone who has ever hurt me, (Name them if you need to.) and I ask you to forgive me for hurting others. I release all hindrances of my past to you, Lord. I release my past, my failures, my sadness, and my hopes and dreams to you.

Thank you Lord for writing a new chapter in my LIFE, and I give you the pen to my book.

Love, In Jesus' name,
Your son or daughter

WORKS CITED

Child Bible Songs. (n.d.). *Child Bible Songs*. Retrieved February 16, 2016, from http://childBiblesongs.com/song-12-be-careful-little-eyes.shtml

Dart, R. (2011, April 06). *Test of a Prophet*. Retrieved March 23, 2016, from icogsfg.org: http://www.icogsfg.org/rld-test-prop.html

Dictionary.com. (2016). *Fruit*. Retrieved August 27, 2015, from Dictionary.com: http://dictionary.reference.com/browse/fruit

Eckhardt, J. (2015, January 20). *Why a Christian Can Have a Demon*. Retrieved March 25, 2 016, from Charisma Magazine: http://www.charismamag.com/spirit/spiritual-growth/846-why-a-christian-can-have-a-demon?showall=&start=1

Ehmann, P. (Composer). (2015). Book of Remembrance. [A. P. Ehmann, Performer] Columbia, KY, USA.

Hunter, C. a. (2002, July). *Angels on Assignmnet*. Retrieved February 18, 2016, from www.angelsonassignment.com/throne_room.html

Kelly, J. P., & Costa, P. (1999). *End Time Warriors*. Gospel Light Publications.

Morgan, B. W. (2010). *Travail and Apostolic Order*. Retrieved February 22, 2016, from Vision International Ministries: http://www.visionintlm.com/apps/articles/default.asp?articleid=66581&columnid=5958

Morris, Henry M. Ph.D. 1998. The Tree Of Life. Acts & Facts. 27 (10).

Murphy, R. (2004). *Words of Blessing, Words of Cursing.* Retrieved February 13, 2016, from Maranatha Life: http://maranathalife.com/teaching/words.htm

Random House Dictionary. (2016). *Dictionary.Reference.com.* Retrieved February 16, 2016, from http://dictionary.reference.com/browse/gardener

Sissom, C. (2016, February 14). *Eastgate.* Retrieved February 14, 2 016, from Eastgate Ministries: http://www.eastgateministries.com/index.php?option=com_content&task=view&id=1017&Itemid=66

Survivor-Manual.com. (n.d.). *Pine Tree Equal Wild Edible Food.* Retrieved March 23, 2016, from Survival-Manual.com: http://www.survival-manual.com/edible-plants/pine.php

Swindoll, C. R. (1994). *The Bride: Renewing our Passion for the Church.* Grand Rapids: Zondervan Publishing House.

Taylor, P. (2012, November 1 9). *The Healing Leaves.* Retrieved March 23, 2016, from FaithWriters.com: http://articles.faithwriters.com/reprint-article-details.php?id=24944

The Holy Bible, English Standard Version Copyright © 2001 by Crossway Bibles, a publishing ministry of Good News Publishers.

The Hub Gathering. (2016, January 9). *YouTube.* Retrieved February 18, 2016, from https://youtu.be/Ow_vVOYASgo

White, M. D. (2013, October 20). Prophet. (T. God's Place in Clarksville, Interviewer)

Wigglesworth, S. (2001). Ever Inceasing Faith. In S. Wigglesworth, *Ever Increasng Faith* (p. 120). Whitaker House.

ABOUT THE AUTHOR

Dr. June Dawn Knight is a mother, grandmother. In addition she serves the Bride as an author, prophetess, and President of TreeHouse Publishers & We are the Bride Ministries.

Her heart is to serve the Body of Christ. She has been in public service for the last 15 years. She spearheaded four organizations. The Middle Tennessee Jr. League Cheerleader's Association in which she unified four different counties and ten cities for cheerleading. She also served as the president of the Steelworker's Union for the CMCSS Bus Drivers in 2004/2005. Then, she went to World Harvest Bible College in Columbus, Ohio. Following Bible College she attended Austin Peay State University from 2008 - 2012. During her time at APSU, she spearheaded three organizations on campus. Dr. June Dawn served student life and served on the Provost Committee for the students.

June Dawn graduated APSU in December 2012 with her Master's Degree in Corporate Communication. She studied in London during Grad School under the top three global Public Relations/Advertising Firms in the world. During this time under the instruction of the University of Kentucky, she made a 100 in the class. She graduated with a 3.74 GPA. June Dawn had dreams of traveling the world for a major corporation, however, after graduation; God stopped her plans and called her back to the ministry.

After submitting 100% to the call of God, she has been serving the Body of Christ in many areas such as websites for pastors, ministries, film, pictures, video, graphic designs, marketing, advertising, etc. She has used her skills to help others. Her heart is to serve the Body of Christ through the direction of the Holy Spirit.

Dr. June Dawn has the revelation that when she obeys the Holy Spirit, that He will take care of her needs and she has this motto, "Obeying the Lord is where your wealth is."

Dr. June Dawn attained her Doctorate in Theology through the International Miracle Institute under the Direction of Dr. Christian Harfouche. This ministry falls under the same lineage as Pastor Rod Parsley, Lester Sumrall, and Smith Wigglesworth.

Dr. June is the author of a series titled, *We are the Bride Series*. The first was released September 2015, *Testimony of a Broken Bride; Jesus is the True Husband*. These Garden Twin books are numbers two and three in the series.

Her previous book, *Selling the Mark of the Beast: Marketing RFID – EU vs. US* was released in January 2015.

For more information go to www.drjune.org, www.gotreehouse.org, or www.wearethebride.us.